So You Th Know the Golden State?

A Story of Northern California Told in 100 Buildings

Doug Gelbert

Cruden Bay Books

SO YOU THINK YOU KNOW THE GOLDEN STATE?
A STORY OF NORTHERN CALIFORNIA TOLD IN 100 BUILDINGS

Cruden Bay Books
184 Kanuga Heights Lane
Hendersonville NC 28739

Introduction

If those walls could talk…this is what they would say. A story about Northern California.

Sardines… Spanish missions… counterculture… trolley parks… Eichler Homes… kissing bridges… Santa Rosa plums… Russian colonization… crime and punishment… camels… lawn bowling… Hetch Hetchy… skiing… blimps… landfills… fire lookouts… big trees… Japanese internment camps… octagon houses… Carnegie libraries… post office murals… Googie architecture… Bear Flag Revolt. This book will have you telling stories like a native in no time.

The photos and stories collected here are a fast and fun way to learn the explanations behind the quirks, the traditions and the secrets that make Northern California uniquely California. Why did California's first railroad use a gauge seen nowhere else? Solved. Where was the largest ship ever constructed on the West Coast built? A mystery no more. Where was the U.S. Hickory Open contested in Northern California? Identified. Where is the world's first reinforced concrete bridge? Revealed.

Imagine a group of settlers arriving in an undeveloped location. First come shelters in which to live and then structures in which to work and shop. There are buildings for worship and education. As the community grows government buildings are required. With prosperity comes places in which to spend leisure time. And each step along the way builds a story only Northern California can call its own. A story told in 100 buildings. Almost all of the selections within are open to the public, or at least visible from public spaces. So, if you haven't seen these landmarks in person, fire up your GPS and get out and see the story of the Golden State standing in plain sight on Northern California streets!

Tuluwat Island
Eureka
prehistoric

Shell middens are found in only a few countries and mostly in America in the Southeast where oyster shells have been carbon-dated to 3,000 years ago. The purpose of their construction is still a bit of a mystery. Middens are assumed to be a refuse heap but why keep piling so high? The shell midden on Tuluwat Island covers six acres and is built 14 feet above the shore - high enough to be seen from the mainland. The creators of the midden were the Wiyot peoples who used the island as a spiritual center. Each year the members of the tribe would gather for a World Renewal Ceremony. Knowing that in 1860, a group of white settlers waited for the men to leave the island to get provisions for the celebration and massacred nearly 100 women and children, using clubs so as not to issue the report of rifles. The destruction of the Tuluwat Village led to the building of a dry dock and boat repair yard which operated for more than a century. After it closed the island has been systematically returned to the Wiyot Tribe by the City of Eureka, including the 4.5 acres remaining of the shell midden, now a National Historic Landmark.

Mission San Carlos
Carmel
1770

The Spanish mission system set up in California in 1769 was a masterclass in colonial bureaucracy. The missions would be established by Catholic priests accompanied by civilian settlers and military personnel to create settlements strung along the Pacific Ocean and knitted together overland for 600 miles by road known as the Camino Real. Before a mission could become a reality a priest needed to wade through months of paperwork at every level of Spanish government. The desired site needed to have an ample supply of fresh water, abundant timber, and terrain favorable for growing crops. There would eventually be 21 missions which account for most of California's oldest structures. Mission San Carlos was the second built by the Franciscans and beginning in 1797 operated as the headquarters for all the Alto California missions. In 1833, after a dozen years of Mexican rule, all the Spanish missions were secularized and most of their extensive lands sold off to the highest bidder. When the Treaty of Guadalupe Hidalgo settled the Mexican American War in 1848 the winning United States honored the church's claim to return mission buildings. San Carlos was in ruins but managed to limp on through the years. In 1931 Harry Downie was on his way to open a cabinet shop in Santa Barbara when he took a job restoring statues at the Carmel mission. He never left. For the next 50 years Downie pored over Spanish source material and scoured the state for period artifacts. Downie left the most authentic representative of the historic California Missions, built around the only original bell and tower in the state.

Presidio of San Francisco
San Francisco
1776

The Presidio of San Francisco was the third and northernmost of the defensive positions established by the Spanish after colonization of Alta California began in 1769. The strategic position south of the entrance to San Francisco Bay was never heavily garrisoned until it came under United States control in the Mexican-American War. The military got busy and The Presidio would be at the center of American involvement in every conflict in the Pacific Rim for the next 150 years. This was the headquarters of the Western Defense Command during World War II and men were deployed for Operation Desert Storm in the 1991 Gulf War. All the while underneath the military activity sat some of the most jaw-droppingly beautiful and valuable land in the country. When the base closed in 1996 an auction loomed but Congress stepped in and established the Presidio Trust to protect 800 buildings, the historic Crissy Field airstrip, and much more. While operating as a recreational paradise for the public the Presidio also maintains a unique residential and commercial leasing operation of the facility.

Royal Presidio Chapel
Monterey
1794

Spanish explorers had been poking around the Pacific Coast from Mexico for the better part of 250 years before Governor Don Gaspar de Portola stood on a hill in San Diego on July 1, 1769 and claimed "Alta California" for Spain. To protect its new territory the Spanish set out to construct four presidios - the first in San Diego, then Monterey, San Francisco and Santa Barbara. Spain and its New World rival England approached colonization differently - where the British saw people already living on the land as impediments to be removed the Spanish considered the indigenous people as potential Catholic converts and eventually citizens - once the appropriate religious and cultural values were absorbed, of course. And also an invaluable labor force. Master stonemason Manuel Ruiz directed his Indian crews to create this ornate replacement for a wooden chapel that had started the Presidio of Monterey in 1770. When Spanish rule ended after barely 50 years in 1821 the Presidio was abandoned and only the finely crafted chapel stood. Two centuries later the Chapel is a rare souvenir of 18th century Spanish architecture and the finest of all Spanish-created religious buildings in California.

Rotchev House
Fort Ross
1812

While French and English fur trappers were penetrating the interior of North America in the 18th century Russian trappers were colonizing the western edge of the continent after Vitus Bering demonstrated it was possible to reach the Pacific Ocean through northern Arctic waters in 1725. There were a score of Russian settlements in the territory claimed in Alaska and several in Hawaii. In 1812 Fort Ross was established in an uninhabited patch of Mexican territory on the Alta California coast as an agricultural community to supply food to the other Pacific outposts. The Russians introduced windmills and ship-building to California; their houses were the first to be constructed entirely of wood and their glass windows had never been seen in Alta California. By the 1830s the Mexican authorities were becoming wary of the Russian presence and granted land to Swiss immigrant-turned Mexican citizen, John Sutter, to counterbalance "hunting and trading companies from the Columbia River." However by this time the supply of otters was proving not to be inexhaustible and Russia was being consumed with troubles at home on the Crimean Peninsula. Fort Ross was sold to Sutter, now an American, in 1849 for $19,788 in "notes and gold" and soon would sell its Alaska claims to the United States for $7.2 million. Fort Ross, the only settlement ever built by Russia in California, is now a state historic park; all the buildings are reconstructions save for the redwood plank house that was the quarters of the commandant. Last occupied by Alexander Rotchev, it is one of only a handful of Russian-built structures in the country.

Custom House
Monterey
1827

The first European to visit Monterey Bay was Spanish explorer Juan Rodríquez Cabrillo in 1542 but there was no hurry to come ashore. It was not until 1770 that the Royal Presidio of Monterey was established and six years later the base became the first capital of both Baja (lower) and Alta (upper) California. Isolated Monterey did not learn about Mexico's independence from Spain until 1822, nearly a year after the fact. Authorities wasted no time switching allegiances and one of the first things the new Mexicans did was open the borders to trade, which Spain had prohibited. Collecting duties on goods was the primary way a territory could fund itself and the Custom House became the first government building in California. Monterey was transforming into a cosmopolitan outpost with ships arriving from America, South America, England and Asia. The United States even set up a consulate, the only one in Alta California. After the Mexican-American War the Stars and Stripes flew for the first time in California over the Custom House. The 1849 Constitution, however, set the first state capital up the coast in San Jose and for the first time Monterey was not a capital city. The Custom House continued to collect taxes until 1868 when the government sold it for private use. Gone, but not forgotten. After the building was abandoned and left to deteriorate the Native Sons of the Golden West targeted it as one of the first conservation projects on the Pacific Coast. After a restoration the Custom House became a museum and the first ever California State Landmark.

Rancho Petaluma
Petaluma
1834

The Spanish began the policy of populating Alta California via land grants. Grants could only be made by the Spanish Crown, however, and title was never included. With Mexican independence the policy changed to give grantees legal title to the land. In 1833 the mission lands set up by Spain were secularized and an additional 8,000,000 acres needed to be transferred into the private hands. Grants became vast and none larger than Rancho Petaluma. Mariano Guadalupe Vallejo, the commander of the Presidio of San Francisco, picked up 66,000 acres and set out to build a combination living quarters and command center for his ranching operations. The Petaluma Adobe would be the largest adobe building ever constructed in California and was not completely finished after ten years when the Mexican-American War erupted. Vallejo was not overly concerned by being on the losing side and enthusiastically persuaded fellow rancheros to embrace American rule. He participated in the California Constitutional Convention and served in the first term of the State Senate in 1850. Meanwhile, his vast land holdings were dissipating. When the newly formed Land Commission met to adjudicate who owned what they faced a pile of 813 land claims. Many would wind through the courts for years. Vallejo sold what he could of Rancho Petaluma in 1857 and lived out the final 33 years of his life at his estate in Sonoma, a town he had laid out in 1835. Petaluma Adobe is now a National Historic Landmark interpreting the era of the Mexican rancheros.

Castro House
San Juan Batista
1838

The José Castro House is one of the best examples of Monterey-styled architecture, a California original blended from Spanish colonial adobe influences and wood frame New England houses. Castro was as powerful a man as could be found in Alta California, serving at various times as governor and commanding general of the Mexican territory, although he harbored California self-rule sentiments above all else. Castro commanded the losing California forces during the Mexican-American War, costing Mexico the northern part of the territory. The well-respected general was then put in charge of the remaining southern section under Mexican control, Baja California. Showing there was no ill will, he offered his fine home to Patrick Breen, the first English-speaking Americans to settle in the area, to live in until he had the money to buy the property. The Breens were twice blessed - the family were survivors of the disastrous Donner Party that lost three dozen members crossing the Sierra Nevadas. Fortune smiled yet again on the family when a Breen son struck it rich in the gold fields, earning enough money to buy the house from Castro in 1854. The Greens stayed until 1935 before selling to the State for the San Juan Bautista State Historical Park.

Sutter's Fort
Sacramento
1843

John Sutter was one of California's earliest settlers and the Golden State may not have produced a more confounding character since. Was he a swindler or a dreadful businessman? Was he a dreamer or a schemer? Was he a manipulator or a bumbler? John Suter emigrated from Switzerland with the most American trait of all - the idea that he could reinvent himself, starting with his name. His main motivation for sailing for the United States in 1834, leaving his family, was to put an ocean between himself and a posse of debt collectors. Sutter dreamed of an agricultural utopia in the West but got sidetracked and wound up in Hawaii and Alaska first. When he finally arrived in California he had ten Sandwich Island natives in tow. Sutter talked his way into a land grant inland, arguing that there were only indigenous people living there. To increase his holdings Sutter took out Mexican citizenship and eventually garnered 300 square miles. With his Hawaiian work force and local Nisenan Indians he constructed Sutter's Fort that became a destination for emigrants on the California Trail. His ranch and farm were filling Sutter's coffers when gold was discovered on his property. Instead of managing the strike Sutter was overwhelmed with land grabbers and was cheated out of most of his property. Soon he was again swamped with debt and his frontier outpost lay in ruins. John Sutter would die 2,500 miles away in Lititz, Pennsylvania in 1880, leaving no money and a complicated legacy. A decade later his frontier fort was resurrected, destined to live on as an historic park.

Sonoma Plaza
Sonoma
1846

In the years following Mexican independence in 1821 the new country's leaders had more pressing concerns than Alta California, nearly a thousand miles away. To encourage settlement generous land grants were given to Mexican citizens and for Europeans and Americans looking for land the process of becoming said citizens was little more than filling out a form or two. This loose arrangement worked well enough for everyone involved until messiness with Texas beginning in 1835 forced Mexican officials to cracked down on non-citizen land grants. With miscommunication rampant, a contingent of about 20 American settlers - maybe with the blessing of U.S. Army Captain John C. Fremont and maybe not - set out on June 14, 1846 to raid horses in the town of Sonoma, home of Commandant General Mariano Vallejo. The town was not garrisoned and the general, who actually favored American rule, even invited the insurgents into his home for wine and a meal. Nonetheless, he was led away to prison at Sutter's Fort where he remained for several weeks. The new overlords needed to raise a flag in Sonoma Plaza so they quickly fashioned a flag with a squat grizzly bear - that appeared more like a pig to those looking up at it - and the grand proclamation of Republic of California. The incident became known as the Bear Flag Revolt but was quickly subsumed in the invasion of Mexico by the United States Army to kickstart the Mexican-American War. The grizzly bear, however, survived to eventually become the official state flag in 1911.

New Almaden
San Jose
1847

The first mining operations in California were not for gold but for mercury. The Ohlone Indians had long used crimson rocks to produce bright body paint but in 1845 Andreas Castillero, a Mexican Army captain trained in metallurgy, recognized the red rocks as cinnabar that could be heated and cooled into quicksilver. Castillero didn't have the resources to properly mine the ore but sold his shares in the land to the English firm of Barron, Forbes, & Company that could. They named the mine New Almaden after the famous mercury mine in Spain. New Almaden would be the largest quicksilver producer after its namesake. There were only so many uses for mercury in the 19th century beyond folk medicines but one of those just happened to be as a gold reducer - handy in the days to come. The New Almaden Mine would go on to generate $70 million worth of mercury - far more than any California gold mine. The towns supporting the mines spread out along the surrounding ridges, housing hundreds of Mexican and Chilean and Spanish miners. The discovery of cyanide as a way to reduce gold ore in 1887 led to a slow decline until the mine shut down in the early 20th century. California's single most lucrative mine became a National Historic Landmark district and a county park with many buildings open for exploration.

Benicia Arsenal
Benicia
1849

Predating California statehood, Benicia was selected as the site for the go-to Army supply base for all West Coast operations, a duty it served until 1964. Today Benicia is one of the most intact historical sites in the Golden State. Included in that roster of original buildings are the Camel Barns, constructed in 1855. The idea of using camels in the inhospitable lands of the southwest first percolated in the 1830s. "They will go without water, and with but little food, for six or eight days, or it is said even longer. Their feet are alike well suited for traversing grassy or sandy plains, or rough, rocky hills and paths, and they require no shoeing...," wrote Lieutenant George Crossman cheerily in a report. The War Department ignored the suggestion until 1853 when Congress appropriated enough money to fund two expeditions to the Mediterranean and return with 70 healthy animals. The camels performed well in tests and on June 25, 1857 a platoon of 25 of the "Camel Corps" set out for Arizona to build a wagon road. The regal "ships of the desert" outperformed their equine counterparts, eating little forage and feasting on desert scrub plants instead. Of course, the camels needed little of the expedition's water. The field reports praised their docility. The military camel experiments disappeared with more pressing matters during the Civil War. With the war won the previous successes were forgotten and the camels sold off, fetching less than $50 a beast. For many years they could be seen in circuses or maybe working as pack animals. Some were released to fend for themselves in the desert. The last of the original Camel Corps, Topsy, was said to have died in the Griffith Park zoo in Los Angeles in 1934.

Alcatraz Island
San Francisco
1850

Alcatraz Island is best known as a federal prison designed to hold "the worst of the worst" of American criminals, depicted in scores and scores of movies, television shows and video games. The Alcatraz Island Prison, closed since 1963 and open for only 30 years, is the reason more than one million tourists visit each year. Yet its time as a federal penitentiary may be the least historically influential period of the existence of "the Island of the Pelicans." Alcatraz was the site of the first American land dispute in the Golden State. Military Governor John C. Fremont bought the island for $5,000 for the United States in 1846 and after winning the Mexican-American War the government declared the island a military reservation. Fremont expected a handsome compensation but received nothing and spent the rest of his life in court trying to get his money back. In 1854 the first lighthouse on the West Coast was erected on Alcatraz Island. The bay's cold, strong currents made Alcatraz an ideal location for detention of soldiers convicted of crimes. Later, captured Confederate soldiers, private citizens accused of treason, and Indians joined the ranks of the confined. In 1907 Alcatraz was anointed the official Western U.S. Military Prison. The stint as America's first maximum-security, minimum-privilege jail began in 1934 and ended when operating costs soared to almost triple the national average. In 1969 college students calling themselves the United Indians of All Tribes occupied Alcatraz for perhaps the most impactful 19 months of the island's history. Their protest helped usher in a new government policy of tribal self-determination, signed by President Richard Nixon.

Fort Mason
San Francisco
1851

For the first 150 years after the United States gained control of San Francisco the government took all the best harbor locations for defensive fortifications. But Confederate gunboats never showed up and Japanese armadas didn't mass outside the Golden Gate. So many of those military installations have closed and the "to-die-for" views have been turned back to the public in the form of parks. Fort Mason is a case in point. The hilltop promontory at San Jose Point affords sweeping views of the bay - the perfect spot for cannons yesterday and Instagram today. For most of its 20th century history Fort Mason was a storage and transportation hub for the nation's Pacific operations; 2/3 of all American troops and half the military cargo filtered through Fort Mason. These days the grounds are more the purview of food trucks than troop carriers. Fort Mason has been recognized as a pioneer in the transformation of military bases; many of the buildings house the Fort Mason Center for Arts & Culture with galleries, museums and theaters. The army mess hall has been replaced by communal restaurants and beer halls with million-dollar views.

Big Four Building
Sacramento
1852

Leland Stanford was 37 years old and oversaw a successful import and export business. Collis Huntington, 40, and Mark Hopkins, 48, ran a thriving hardware business. Charles Crocker, aged 39, was a financier. These were the men engineer Theodore Judah convinced to form the Central Pacific Railroad that would cosntruct the Transcontinental Railroad, meeting up the Union Pacific building out from Omaha, Nebraska. As per the Pacific Railway Act of 1862 each company would receive 6,400 acres of land and $48,000 in government bonds for each mile of track laid. None of the Sacramento merchants had any experience with railroads, engineering, or construction. In fact Judah was planning on buying out the "Associates" but contracted yellow fever on his way across Panama and died. He had been heading for New York City to arrange alternate financing. The hardware store became the command center for the Central Pacific. Stanford, who became governor of California in 1862, handled the company political interests in the West; Huntington spent his time in the East courting politicians and moneymen; Crocker was in charge of construction; Hopkins ("he knew how to squeeze 106 cents out of every dollar") was Treasurer. The Transcontinental Railroad, considered an impossible dream a decade before, was completed in 1869. Each of the Central Pacific directors, known to history as "The Big Four," entered the pantheon of America's richest men. By then the company offices had moved to San Francisco. Huntington & Hopkins Hardware continued to operate into the 1900s but eventually the building fell into disrepair. After being recognized as a national Historic Landmark the sagging structure was revived to become a centerpiece of Old Town Sacramento.

Pony Express Terminal
Sacramento
1852

No event of less consequence has been more romanticized in American history than the Pony Express. Or maybe the image of a lone rider, with nothing to guide him but his guts and guile, racing across 2000 miles of empty country solely in pursuit of commerce is the ultimate American symbol. Time is always money and in the mid-19th century overland delivery of mail from the Mississippi River to the Pacific Ocean required 24 days minimum. William Russell, Alexander Majors, and William Waddell had wrapped up most of that delivery of freight to U.S. Army outposts but they believed a satchel of mail could make the trip in just 10 days with a horse shuttle. The men bought a herd of 400 horses and built 184 way stations between St. Joseph, Missouri and Sacramento. They began recruiting lightweight riders, offering $125 a month in pay when a good day's work might bring only a dollar. The first letters went out on April 3, 1860 and indeed reached Sacramento in the terminal in Hastings Bank 10 days later. In 18 months, however, the Pony Express was kaput, done in by the arrival of the telegraph and financial losses. At a time when U.S. postage was two cents the Pony Express started by charging $5.00 a letter. The price eventually fell to $1.00 but the operators could never make the numbers work. Still only one mail pouch was ever lost and only four riders were ever documented to have lost their lives - to Indian attacks - on the job. It was actually more dangerous to work alone in one of the remote express stations. The mythmaking began almost immediately and the Pony Express has been celebrated in movies and television and novels; the route through eight states has been designated a National Historic Trail.

United States Mint
San Francisco
1854

On a lazy Sunday in 1799 Conrad Reed played hooky from church and went down to splash in Little Meadow Creek on the family farm in North Carolina. That day young Conrad found a shiny yellow rock and brought it home. Purported to weigh 17 pounds, for several years it served as a doorstop in the Reed house until a local jeweler recognized the rock as gold. America's first gold rush was on. By 1824 John Reed had collected an estimated $100,000 worth of gold from his creek. The government opened its first branch of the main U.S. Mint in Philadelphia to process the ore into coins in 1838. Gold fever struck again that year in Dahlonega, Georgia and another branch was built. So the U.S. Treasury was old hands at this gold rush business when word came of strikes in California. But America had never seen anything like this - $4 million dollars in gold coins were minted in San Francisco in the first year. That was about four times as much as the Charlotte Mint coined in its 23-year history. Almost immediately a new building was on the drawing board. A block-swallowing Greek temple came online in 1874 and put in six decades of service before it too was replaced. All three San Francisco branches of the United States Mint still stand.

Mare Island Navy Yard
Vallejo
1854

Thanks to his father, David Glasgow Farragut signed on as a midshipman in the U.S. Navy at the age of nine. Two years later he was fighting in the War of 1812. The next 40 years of Farragut's naval career were relatively mundane until he received the assignment in 1854 to oversee construction of the first American naval base on the Pacific Coast. Captain Farragut officially commissioned Mare Island on July 16, 1858. Shortly thereafter Farragut was in the Civil War where his heroics on the Mississippi River and Mobile Bay propelled him to become the first Admiral in United States history. Mare Island's star was on the rise as well. The USS *Saginaw*, a paddle-wheel gunboat, was launched on March 3, 1859, the first of over 500 ships birthed in the shipyard. In 1872 work was begun on the first dry dock in the West. It would take 19 years and countless granite blocks to complete but Dry Dock 1 remains one of the most impressive feats of stone masonry ever attempted. Mare Island was now the premier repair depot for the Navy on the Pacific Coast; if it could float it could be handled in Vallejo. Wartime production was a Mare Island specialty. The USS *Ward*, a destroyer, was built in a record 17 1/2 days during World War I; she would go on to fire the first American shots of World War II when sinking a Japanese midget sub in the early morning hours of December 7, 1941. In 1919 the battleship USS *California* slid into the Mare Island waters as the largest ship ever constructed on the West Coast. During World War II some 46,000 civilian and military personnel worked at Mare Island making crucial repairs on battled-damaged ships. After the war, Mare Island converted to submersibles, producing 17 nuclear-powered submarines. The naval yard shuttered in 1996 after 142 years, shifting to a future civilian life.

Empire Mine
Grass Valley
1854

The gold that triggered the California Gold Rush was placer gold, deposits in the sand and gravel of stream beds. It did not take long for this "easy gold" to play out. What followed was hard rock mining - men lowered in buckets through shafts to drill holes and blast rock into ore cars with black powder. Prospectors fresh off the stagecoaches were not fit for this kind of work - experienced miners needed to be imported. After gold-bearing quartz was found in the Grass Valley Cornishmen from England were brought to the Empire Mine to build tunnels and pump mine shafts clear of groundwater. The Empire Mine didn't begin sniffing profits until the 1870s. Eventually 367 miles of underground shafts would be dug here. The Gold Rush 49ers were a distant memory when the Empire finally closed after more than 100 years of operation in the 1950s. The haul brought to the surface in that time was 5.8 million ounces of gold, worth about 12 billion dollars in 2024 money.

Arcata and Mad River RR
Blue Lake
1854

The California State Railroad Museum, organized in Sacramento in 1937, is one of the world's great railroad museums. Some of the most powerful steam and diesel locomotives ever built are on display. The Sacramento Valley Railroad was the first to be incorporated in California, on August 4, 1852. But right of way issues meant that the Golden State's first operating railroad began 300 miles from the state capital. The shoreline of the Humboldt Bay was mucky and to facilitate schooners loading lumber the the Union Plank Walk, Rail Track, and Wharf Company built a pier out into the water with redwood timbers as rails. California's first train cars were pulled by horses. At the time there were at least 150 railroads in America and there was a raging debate over the "standard" gauge, the distance between rails. Should it be 4 feet 8 1/2 inches? Or 5 feet? Wider? The builders at the port of Arcata paid no mind - their gauge was set at 3 feet 9 1/4 inches. The story goes that was the width of the first set of wheels they found to use. Despite its rudimentary beginnings the railroad survived - even prospered - until the 1930s. The line eventually stretched almost to eight miles and featured four steam locomotives. After it became Arcata and Mad River RR the service tied into the Northwestern Pacific mainline in 1914. Traces of California's pioneering railroad still exist, including the depot building in Blue Lake, now a museum.

Point Pinos Lighthouse
Pacific Grove
1855

On September 28, 1850, by an Act of Congress, $90,000 was appropriated for "a lighthouse at Alcatraz Island, for a lighthouse at Point Conception and a fog signal, for a lighthouse at Battery Point entrance of the Bay of San Francisco, for a lighthouse at San Diego, for a lighthouse and fog signal at Monterey, for a lighthouse at Farallones off the harbor of San Francisco and a fog signal." These would be the first six lighthouses erected on the West Coast. All were to be fashioned in the style of a New England cottage and all were to be completed by the first of November 1853. Low bidders on the contract were Francis Kelly and Francis Gibbons of Baltimore and it took them more than a year to assemble all the material and hire the bricklayers, carpenters, blacksmiths, masons and other craftsmen for the trip around South America to California. The ship did not pull into San Francisco Bay until December 1852. Alcatraz was up first but the light was replaced in 1909 to accommodate the penitentiary on the island so the oldest continually operating lighthouse of the four dozen or so beacons illuminating California's 800 miles of coastline today is at Point Pinos where even the third-order Fresnel ones ground in France is original. The lighthouse sending a beam 17 miles into the tricky southern approach to Monterey Bay utilized civilian keepers, several who stayed on the job for over 20 years, until 1960.

James Marshall Cabin
Coloma
1856

It was inevitable that Americans would eventually cross the country to live in California in large numbers. Too much good climate, too much natural resources, too much opportunity. Of course no one could imagine that 400,000 people would come at once within months of the United States winning the Alta California Territory in the Mexican-American War. Mexican officials likely shed few tears as they signed the Treaty of Guadalupe Hidalgo on February 2, 1848 and waved goodby to about 7,000 settlers living in a widely dispersed string of mission towns. What no one at the peace talks knew was that on January 24 James Marshall had found some shiny flakes - nothing much more than a quarter of an ounce - in a tailrace he was building at John Sutter's sawmill. Small amounts of gold had been discovered in California before without any attention but in American hands President James K. Polk made public note of this find. The next year there were 100,000 people, dubbed "forty-niners" in the press, poking around California. American territories in the 19th century needed 60,000 inhabitants to petition for statehood and most required decades to get a star on the flag. California became the 31st state in the Union without ever organizing as a territory. The Gold Rush was like nothing the country had seen before or ever saw again. In its first census in 1860 California had 379,994 residents, 26th among all states. Gold fever eventually chilled - California did not crack the nation's Top 20 states for population until 1910. Neither John Sutter nor James Marshall became rich. Marshall built this unassuming cabin in 1856 where he lived until 1870. Penniless most of his life, Marshall was awarded a small pension from the California State Legislature in 1872.

Hendy Iron Works
Sunnyvale
1856

A truism of gold rushes is that the ones who really strike it rich are the ones selling to the miners. Enter Joshua Hendy. Born in England, Hendy sailed for America at the age of 14 as a blacksmith apprentice. After stints in shops in Massachusetts, South Carolina and Texas he was on a boat "'round the horn" and headed for California at the age of 27. After looking at the gold fields Hendy concluded that the giant trees were a better bet than the streams and mines and started a commercial redwood sawmill in Benicia. In 1856 he moved to San Francisco to open the Hendy Machine Works. Hendy fabricated innovative hydraulic equipment for the mining industry that became must-haves as the easy gold disappeared. When mining revenue waned Hendy machines became indispensable in the sawmill and dairy industries. By the time of his death in 1891 his machine shop occupied a full city block near the Embarcadero. The 1906 Earthquake destroyed the Hendy Iron Works and nephews Samuel and John took Sunnyvale up on an offer of free land to rebuild the plant along the Southern Pacific Railroad hard by the San Francisco Bay. The machine shop pivoted quickly to military production in World War I and even more so in World War II when 11,500 employees churned out critical parts for the nation's fleet of cargo-bearing Liberty Ships. After that effort Hendy Iron Works was absorbed into Westinghouse Electric and later Northrop Grumman as the plant became exclusively a defense production facility. The old Hendy administration building out front carries on as a museum.

Bidwell Bar Bridge
Oroville
1856

Suspension bridges are one of our oldest forms of bridge-building, dating back to the 1400s when Thangtong Gyalpo used iron chains to hang decks around Tibet and Bhutan. The first wire-cable suspension bridge in the United States, just a temporary footbridge in Philadelphia, did not appear until 1796. Suspension bridges did not become widespread until German engineer John Roebling started specializing in the technique in the 1840s; he would culminate his career with the Brooklyn Bridge in the 1880s. California got its first suspension bridges in gold country over the Feather River. The elements for the Bidwell Bar Bridge needed to be manufactured by the Starbuck Iron Works in Troy, New York, shipped around the Cape of Good Horn and hauled overland for assembly. The final tab was $34,922. Before the bridge opened to traffic a ferry collected 25 cents to cross on foot and $2.00 for a heavy wagon. The bridge carried traffic until the 1960s when it was replaced by what was the third highest suspension bridge in the world at the time - although when the Lake Oroville Reservoir is filled the span sits just above the water level. California's oldest remaining suspension bridge was taken apart and reassembled at the south end of the lake.

State Capitol
Sacramento
1860

After California was granted statehood and following intense lobbying at the Constitutional Convention, San Jose became the first capital. Town leaders hastily purchased a two-story hotel under construction to accommodate the state legislature but an unusually wet winter delayed progress on the building. After holding senate sessions in private houses and slogging through knee-deep muddy streets the disgruntled legislators voted to move the capital from San Jose before the third session convened. California's first capitol building was left vacant and consumed by fire in 1853. The following year Sacramento was tabbed as the permanent capital. Not that the matter was settled in everybody's eyes. There would be talk about moving well into the 1900s from places like Berkeley and San Jose and Monterey but after 170 years the matter now seems likely settled - Sacramento is the sixth largest city in California with 525,000 people and over 70,000 of them work for the state government. Reuben Clark, leaning heavily on the United States Capitol building for inspiration, drew up the plans for the California State Capitol.

Charles Krug Winery
Saint Helena
1861

George Calvert Yount's grave in the town that bears his name has been recognized as a California Historical Landmark, attributing to him "all the finest qualities of an advancing civilization blending with the existing primitive culture." The historic citation makes no mention of growing the first grapes in Napa Valley. The North Carolina-born Yount was a cattleman by trade but in 1825 after a neighbor embezzled his savings he headed West as a trapper. Yount is said to be the first American citizen to declare Mexican citizenry and receive a generous land grant to settle the northern Alta California frontier. By the time he got around for sending for his wife in 1841 she had married someone else. Prussian emigrant Charles Krug built the Valley's first commercial winery in 1861 which became the model for 140 fellow California vintners in the next few decades. The good times stopped rolling in the early 1900s when a ravenous root louse gobbled 80% of Napa's vines and then the national Volstead Act banned any beverage in the country with more than one half percent alcohol for 15 years. To help rejuvenate the wine business seven local winegrowers banded together in 1944 to move forward as the Napa Valley Vintners. If ever a trade association enjoyed a watershed moment it was in Paris, France in 1976. Playing the role of David on Goliath's home turf two California wineries scored top honors in the blind taste tests, rocketing Napa Valley to oenophilic superstardom. Today's Napa Valley Vinters includes more than 500 wineries and an international reputation for excellence.

McElroy House
San Francisco
1861

Orson Squire Fowler was responsible for two wildly different fads in the middle of the 19th century. One was phrenology, the practice that mental acuity could be determined by the bumps on one's head. The other was eight-sided houses that he championed in a book called *The Octagon House, A Home for All*. Neither are much in vogue these days but the octagon at least made sense. The houses offered a greater space-to-surface ratio and thus were cheaper to construct than rectangular houses. You could get more interior light and greater cross-ventilation, both important considerations in the days before electricity. But the lack of square corners would play havoc with interior designers. Octagons enjoyed a loger popularity with barns where furntiure wasn't as much of an issue. Following Fowler's book like a YouTube how-to video William and Harriet McElroy tackled their new eight-sider in a rural area of San Francisco known as Cow Hollow. The final product looks to be a reproduction of "The Best Plan Yet" from Fowler's 1853 book. The house stayed in the McElroy family until the 1920s. The National Society of the Colonial Dames of America rescued the deteriorating redwood octagon in 1952 and operate it as a house museum.

Bridgeport Covered Bridge
Bridgeport
1862

Covered bridges are the favorites of romantics everywhere. Wooden bridges were, however, the apogee of practicality - the roof protect- ed the structural elements from the weather. It is estimated that over 14,000 covered transportation bridges have been constructed in the United States and fewer than 1,000 remain. California boasts ten "kissing bridges" - a half dozen from the 19th century days of horse-drawn buggies and buckboards. The Bridgeport Covered Bridge was constructed by sawmill owner David Wood with some urgency. The first major discovery of silver in the United States had recently been discovered by Henry Comstock in Virginia City, Nevada and the Virginia City Turnpike Company needed a toll road built to San Francisco pronto. Wood created a unique bridge with an auxiliary Burr Arch in the center of a Howe Truss; the design would become a model for fellow California bridge builders. The 233-foot span over the South Yuba River has survived - thanks to a recent million-dollar restoration - to not only be one of the oldest covered bridges in the Golden State but the longest single span covered bridge anywhere.

Summit Tunnel
Donner Pass
1865

An estimated 400,000 settlers headed west on the Oregon Trail beginning in the 1840s. Almost all survived wherever it was they decided to end up. For those headed to California the jump-off point of the Trail was in today's southern Idaho. Even though the 2,100-mile wagon road was well established almost from the get-go there were always ideas on how to conquer the journey quicker. Lansford Hasting was one who had a better way to get to California by leaving the Oregon Trail earlier, from Fort Bridger in Wyoming. Two families he persuaded were the Reeds and the Donners from Indiana in 1846. The Hastings Cutoff had never been attempted with wagons and undue delays kept the Donner Party from traversing a 7,056-foot pass through the Sierra Nevadas before snowfall. Forced to overwinter in one of the snowiest spots in the Western Hemisphere only 48 of the 87 members of the pioneer caravan were alive to be rescued the following spring. While most of the mountain passes in California were named for their discoverers Donner Pass assumed the name of unluckiest of Golden State-bound settlers. The Donner cabins were already tourist attractions of sorts when the Central Pacific Company arrived in 1865 to complete their side of the Transcontinental Railroad. The Central Pacific would build 15 tunnels through the Sierras but all paled in difficulty to the Summit Tunnel on the Donner Pass - 1/3 of a mile through solid granite. Thousands of Chinese workers were hired through contractors who recruited men directly from China, some with knowledge of gunpowder that was, save for back-breaking labor, the only tool available for the job. Some days progress under snow sheds would be measured in inches but the Chinese crews wrapped up work on the tunnels in a staggering 16 months, more than a year-and-a-half ahead of schedule. The tunnel was abandoned in 1993 but is still accessible to hikers.

Nevada Theatre
Nevada City
1865

In the final decades of the 19th century most communities boasted an opera house although its function was often for just about everything except opera. Townsfolk would come to enjoy lectures, watch pageants and graduations and patronize live performances. Among those who graced the stage in Nevada City were Mark Twain, Jack London and the revered star of the California mining camps, Lotta Crabtree. Lotta arrived in California from New York with her family when she was six years old in 1853. Soon she was dancing and singing and playing the banjo for entertainment-starved miners. By the time she moved to San Francisco a decade later she owned her own theatrical company. When Crabtree appeared in Nevada City the audiences were in the thousands. "The San Francisco Favorite" headed to the East Coast where she became "The Nation's Darling" and America's best paid actress. The Nevada Theatre went through a period in the 1900s as a movie house but has been restored as a stage befitting California's oldest existing theater building.

Fort Bidwell

Fort Bidwell
1865

In the matter of "taming" the American West there was always a theory, never predominant, that is was easier to sublimate the indigenous peoples with books rather than bullets. The idea of "cultural assimilation" goes all the way back to George Washington. After 1880 the federal government eventually banned all traditional Indian religious practices and established boarding schools where children were forced off their reservations and required to speak English. "Kill the Indian, save the man," was the government credo. Their success was a mixed bag. Demand for some Indian schools outstripped capacity, attracting students from distant tribes. Sports were played at high levels and some students matriculated into colleges and jobs. Others devolved into cheap labor camps, rife with student abuses. California had three Indian Boarding Schools. Fort Bidwell Indian School was the last to open, in 1898, and the first to close, in 1930. St. Boniface Indian Industrial School in Banning was the first, operating from 1890 until 1952; all its buildings were demolished in 1974. The Perris Indian School opened in 1892 and moved to the Sherman Institute in Riverside in 1903; the school still operates as Sherman Indian High School, part of the state educational system with 70% of the student body drawn from local reservations. All left complicated legacies for individual students behind their shuttered doors. What cannot be denied, however, is that they were the only schools ever set up by the government to erase the culture of an entire people. At Fort Bidwell each October California Indian Day Celebration honors the Fort Bidwell Indian Boarding School Elders.

Knight Foundry
Sutter Creek
1872

Water has been used for power for centuries but Gold Rush miners in the West faced challenges unknown by their American predecessors in the East. California streams often lacked reliable year-round flow. To compensate, resourceful miners developed a system of hydraulic mining that sent water from collection vats plummeting down hundreds of feet of flumes to concentrate the stream into an impulse water wheel. The problem was that water splashed out of the revolving buckets, sapping efficiency from the system. Samuel Knight improved the operation with metal buckets and a patented single-piece cast iron wheel in 1875 which quickly won favor in the mining fields. His foundry grew into the largest outside of San Francisco, keeping 44 workers busy. While working with a Knight wheel millwright Lester Pelton watched a bucket slip out of position and the wheel actually pick up speed when struck by the jet. Pelton tinkered with dozens of configurations until developing a split bucket water wheel that he unveiled in an Idaho Mining Company trial. Pelton's wheel operated at 90.2% efficiency to the Knight wheel's 76.5%. The Pelton Wheel became the prototype for massive turbines used in modern hydroelectric power generation. Lester Pelton became rich, inducted into the National Inventors Hall of Fame, and was featured in a television episode of *Death Valley Days*. The Pelton Wheel is also why we have the Knight Foundry today, an industrial 19th century treasure. Samuel Knight continued inventing and manufacturing equipment and the foundry would remain in business until 1996. But there was never a wild success that necessitated modernization, nor did a succession of owners feeling the urge to upgrade the operation. So the Knight Foundry survives as a rare original worksite from America's early days of water power.

South Hall
Berkeley
1873

In 1862 in the midst of the Civil War Justin Morrill, a representative from Vermont, served up one of the most impactful bills ever introduced in Congress. The Morrill Land-Grant College Act of 1862 divided up 11 million acres of Western lands to give to states to sell and use the proceeds to endow "at least one college" for scientific studies. Each state received 30,000 acres for each member of Congress; being only 12 years old California pocketed 150,000 acres. The bounty was ticketed for the Agricultural, Mining, and Mechanical Arts College when actual money showed up in the bank. Meanwhile trustees of a newly chartered College of California had bought farms north of Oakland facing the Golden Gate that had strained their resources. A school without money and a pool of money without a school. The legislature welded the two together under the banner of University of California in 1868. North and South Halls, to house the College of Letters and the College of Agriculture, were the first two buildings planned for campus. The wrecking ball claimed North Hall in 1917, leaving South Hall as the only souvenir of the University of California-Berkeley's original core of buildings. The ornate Second Empire design is a vivid reminder of how the West deferred to Eastern tastes in all things cultural until finding its own footing in the 1900s.

Cable Railway
San Francisco
1873

In 1852 Andrew Smith bought an interest in a Mariposa County gold mine and left his native Scotland with his 16-year old son Andrew to investigate. What he found was not promising and the next year Smith was back in Scotland. But Andrew, who would adopt the surname of his inventor uncle Andrew Hallidie, remained to work in the gold fields. Dad may have left too soon. Young Andrew observed that the ropes used to pull ore cars in the hills were often not up to the job. Using wire rope patented by his father Hallidie employed cables laid between the tracks to ease cars down the slopes. The cars gripped the cable as needed and were pulled along by machinery. Andrew Smith Hallidie saw more dollar signs in the cable than the ore in the cars and left for San Francisco to manufacture wire rope. In 1873 Hallidie introduced the first cable cars to San Francisco on the notoriously steep Clay Street. There were other grip car transportation systems around, most notably in New York City and Chicago, which operated the largest and most profitable cable car system in America. But other places didn't have San Francisco's severe hills and cities found it easier to just use electrified trolleys when the technology became available. Meanwhile the Clay Street Hill Railroad was just the beginning in San Francisco where there would be 23 cable car lines by the time of Hallidie's death at the age of 64 in 1900. Three routes of the world's last manually operated cable car system remain today: one along California Street and two running from Union Square to Fisherman's Wharf. Since the cable cars only travel in one direction when the cars reach the end of the line a gripman manually rotates the car on a turntable for the return trip.

Burbank House
Santa Rosa
1875

Nowhere is a seller's reputation of more paramount importance than the seed business. To the consumer an ill-bred seed looks exactly like the blue-ribbon winner. Not until the plant actually grows months later will the buyer know if he has made a good bargain. As a young man in Massachusetts Luther Burbank developed a potato which he sold the rights to produce for $150 in 1875. Burbank used the money to skedaddle all the way across the country and went into the nursery business. Burbank built a good reputation but his passion lay as a hybridizer of plants, not a merchant. His experiments in Santa Rosa attracted the support of moneymen like Andrew Carnegie and Thomas Edison and Burbank went on to introduce over 800 new plants to the world. Significantly for California agriculture, and therefore everyone, Burbank focused on crop plants, fruits and nuts. He was fastidious in his methods, growing 10,000 plants at a time and selecting a handful of seeds to produce the next batch of 10,000 until his efforts bore the fruits he desired. The work in the Santa Rosa experimental farm became the backbone for modern plant genetics and breeding. Henry Ford packed up Burbank's garden office and moved it to his collection of Americana in Michigan but his home and garden of 52 years became a park and museum. And that original Burbank potato? The Russet Burbank is the most widely grown potato in America.

Wawona Hotel
Wawona
1876

Canadian-born Galen Clark jumped into the California Gold Rush in 1854 after his wife died when he was 40 years old. Instead of finding gold he contracted tuberculosis. His doctor gave him the proverbial six months to live so he headed for the mountains where he figured his prospects for survival would be "about even." He became the first non-indigenous person to see and write about giant sequoias, the largest living organisms on earth. Clark immediately began agitating for the sequoia's protection and in 1864 President Abraham Lincoln signed preservation legislation for the Mariposa Grove "to be left in-alienable for all time." The rambling Wawona Hotel was built for tour-ists visiting the magnificent trees. "Preservation" was a different animal in the 19th century - one of the first things done for visitors to the Mar-iposa Grove was to bore a hole through the 26-foot diameter of the Wawona Tree for carriages in 1881. The world's first "tunnel tree" was joined by a half-dozen others, including the California Tunnel Tree in the Mariposa Grove in 1895. When the National Park Service formed in 1916 the tunnel trees were promoted as stars for the new parks. At least Galen Clark didn't have to bear witness to the degradation; he had died in 1910 at the age of 95, surviving a half-century beyond his assumed death sentence. The Wanona, now in Yosemite National Park, is still a base for big tree hunting.

Saloon
Bodie
1877

There had not been a really big gold strike in California for more than 20 years when word spread in 1876 of a mine cave-in north of Mono Lake that uncovered a juicy vein of ore. Dreams die hard. The population of Bodie jumped from a few dozen to an estimated 5,000 by 1880. There were more than 2,000 structures in town. It looked like W.S. Bodey had imagined after he had made a minor strike in the area in 1859. The town never grew after that but Bodey also never suffered the disappointment - he perished in a blizzard the winter after his discovery. Now Bodie had 65 saloons, a red light district and enough brawls and holdups to provide steady salacious fodder for the several newspapers in town. There was even a Chinatown. But there wasn't that much gold. People were drifting away by 1881 and the population was under 800 by the end of the decade. The mine limped along into the 1940s after which Bodie descended into "ghost town" territory. In 1962 the legislature created Bodie State Historic Park. The 170 or so buildings that remained were preserved in a state of "arrested decay," looking exactly as they did when abandoned, right down to inventories remaining on store shelves.

Embarcadero Seawall
San Francisco
1879

In the 1840s you could literally use your fingers to count the ships that entered San Francisco harbor each year. In the first full year of the Gold Rush in 1849 there were 650 vessels vying for space to tie up on shore. It is believed that at least 500 ships were just grounded in the mud flats and abandoned while everybody headed for the gold fields. San Francisco needed a waterfront. Private money jumped in first but a more co-ordinated effort by the State created the Port of San Francisco. Job One was building a seawall. A trench was dug in the mud flats and filled with rock and rubble and eventually topped with concrete. Work continued until 1916 when three miles of seawall had been constructed, defining the footprint of the waterfront. More than 500 acres of marshland were converted into some of the most valuable land in America along the Embarcadero. From Fisherman's Wharf to Mission Creek, the Embarcadero Seawall has literally held San Francisco together for over 100 years. In that time the water level in San Francisco Bay has risen 8 inches; some prognosticators say in the next hundred it will rise five feet. The seawall and San Francisco will be a very different place if that happens.

Chautauqua Hall
Pacific Grove
1881

In a wildly productive life Lewis Miller registered 92 patents but it was the Buckeye Mower and Reaper that made him rich. A devout Methodist, in 1874 he founded the Chautauqua Institution in western New York to better train Sunday school teachers. The center's summer programs expanded to include lectures on the arts, culture and outdoor recreation. The Chautauqua ideal for adult education became a phenomenon with thousands of tent camps sprouting across rural America. The Chautauquas had their own magazine and rivaled vaudeville as an entertainment circuit for lecturers who were the live act rock stars of the day. Teddy Roosevelt opined that Chautauqua, with its emphasis on self and civic improvement, is "typically American in that it is typical of America at its best." At the peak of the movement in the 1920s the total yearly audience in Chautauqua tent camps was said to be 45 million. The first Chautauqua in the West was organized in 1879 at Pacific Grove and was such a success that the Southern Pacific Railroad bankrolled the building of Chautauqua Hall. The railroad profited from the thousands of visitors who used its trains to reach the world famous "Chautauqua-by-the-Sea" and the town was soon the western headquarters for the movement. The Chautauquas fizzled out by the 1940s although a few remain; the hall has been restored for dances and concerts.

Sheriff's Gallows
Downieville
1885

Crime was an American spectator sport in the 1800s. Hangings were public spectacles and people would make a day of it, toting picnic lunches to the gallows. In the 1820s the Eastern State Penitentiary in Philadelphia was far and away the most expensive prison ever built, created around the principle of solitary confinement that kept prisoners from seeing each other and, the thinking went, prevent them from sharing their underworld secrets. Thousands of visitors showed up at Eastern State to watch the condemned men at hard labor. In the late 1800s prisons were elaborately designed, attracting tourists whose fears about lawless, uncontrolled inmates plotting dangerous escapes inside could be calmed. These gallows were only used once, on November 27, 1885 to execute 20-year old James O'Neill for the murder of his employer in an argument. It was the last legal hanging in Sierra County as state law ended local executions in 1891 and moved them behind prison walls. The State would end capital punishment in 2006 after putting 513 prisoners to death by hanging (the last in 1941), lethal gas and lethal injection. Back in Downieville the gallows had been dismantled, placed in storage and forgotten. They were re-discovered in 1927 and rebuilt in the courtyard "as a reminder of California's colorful criminal past" where California Registered Historical Landmark No. 971 continues to reside. The folks in Sierra County were prescient about the public's interest in crime - when Alcatraz Island was opened to visitors the old federal prison became one of the biggest tourist attractions in the state.

Carson Mansion
Eureka
1885

Thanks to environmental concerns and their popularity for recreation the thirst for California timber has cooled considerably. These days Golden State forests produce about 350 million board feet annually. In his heyday, William Coleman Carson, the first timber baron to mill redwood, would ship 15 million board feet himself. What better way to advertise your lumber than to construct a glorious wooden home. Carson hired fellow Canadian Samuel Newsom for the job. Newsom tapped just about every Victorian architectural style of the 1880s for his design - Italianate, Queen Anne, Eastlake and Stick. While Carson utilized mostly his own company's redwood for his 18-room house he also provided his army of craftsmen white mahogany from Central America and onyx from Asia to carve. "If I build it poorly, they would say I was a damned miser; if I build it expensively, they will say I am a show-off...guess I'll just build it to suit myself," Carson is reported to have said about his project. Two years and $80,000 later the house was ready; three years after that Carson gifted his showcase to his son as a wedding present. In 1950 local businessmen purchased the house for a men's club that has preserved the house in meticulous detail. So much so the Carson Mansion is touted as the most photographed Victorian house in America. It is also a testament to why milled Victorian houses fell out of favor - the cost of maintenance would drain most any homeowner's bank account.

Flood Mansion
San Francisco
1886

Of all 44 of San Francisco's hills, Nob Hill was the most desirable for a house. It was centrally located and it had the best views. And at 376 feet above the waterfront it offered a refuge from the bawdiness of the unwashed masses below. In fact, the name "Nob" is reputedly a contraction of the Hindu word "nabob" which meant a wealthy or powerful person. The first of those nabobs came with riches from the gold fields when there was just sandy scrub covering the hill. The defining mansions of Nob Hill were built by all four of the railroad barons of the Central Pacific Railroad who engineered the Transcontinental Railroad - Collis Huntington, Leland Stanford, Mark Hopkins and Charles Crocker. They were followed to Nob Hill by two of the "Bonanza Kings" from Nevada's Comstock Lode, James Flood and James Fair, spreading money from America's biggest silver strike. The mansions on the hill in the 1870s were something to behold. Commoners would trudge up the steep sides of Nob Hill - almost a 25% grade on the south side - just to take a look. When adventure novelist Robert Louis Stevenson came to town for a visit in 1882 he called it "the hill of palaces." California's finest homes were no match for the San Francisco Earthquake of 1906 that left only Flood's Connecticut brownstone mansion standing - all the others had been built out of wood.

Alvord Bridge
San Francisco
1889

Concrete is the most widely used building material in the world, so common it is second only to water as the most utilized substance on the planet. But it required the most costly earthquake in American history to convince folks concrete had a future. English-born architect Ernest L. Ransome was the earliest cheerleader for building with reinforced concrete, patenting a system for twisted iron rods set in ferro-concrete in 1884. He erected the first reinforced concrete building in the United States that year for Arctic Oil Works in San Francisco. No one came knocking on his door to ask to build another. Five years later he engineered the first reinforced concrete bridge in America in Golden Gate Park. Ransome even went so far as to improve the appearance by scoring the concrete to resemble sandstone blocks. Still no one cared. With the lack of commissions he packed up his shingle and departed for the East Coast. Ernest Ernest Ransome was 62 years old when the San Andreas Fault slipped for 42 seconds. Eighty percent of the buildings in San Francisco were destroyed. While masonry structures crumbled around the city Ransome's tiny collection of reinforced concrete buildings all remained standing.

Cypress Lawn Memorial Park
Colma
1892

For tourists the 19th century equivalent of today's Yosemite or Yellowstone was Mount Auburn Cemetery in Massachusetts. Before Mount Auburn burials took place on private estates or in downtown graveyards that were anything but permanent. If new development came along cemeteries would be ripped out and moved to a less crowded part of the city. Jacob Bigelow, a Boston physician, saw congested city burial grounds as a health nuisance. It was his idea to build permanent resting places outside the city on landscaped grounds, a rural cemetery if you will. The Rural Cemetery movement caught on in major cities across the country, most of which had never had public parks before. Folks of all classes could come to the cemeteries and enjoy nature, picnic, and stroll through sculpture gardens. All for free. Lone Mountain in San Francisco swallowed the rural cemetery playbook whole when the cemetery opened in 1854, right down to naming sections after famous Eastern prototypes like Mount Auburn and Green-Wood in Brooklyn. In 1867 the entire graveyard took the name of Laurel Hill from Philadelphia. By that time the Catholics, the Odd Fellows and the Masons all had their own cemeteries on Lone Mountain. San Francisco began outlawing new burials in the city in the early 1900s and in the 1920s began relocating graves from Lone Mountain to Cypress Lawn Memorial Park in Colma, a town founded specifically for burials in rural cemeteries. The remains of 150,000 bodies were moved. Each relocation cost $10 for a grave and marker. If the fee wasn't paid the final destination was a mass grave.

Sutro Baths
San Francisco
1894

The concept of leisure was not a part of most American lives until after the Civil War. Entrepreneurs were quick to begin jostling for that new spare time. Among the most popular diversions were trolley parks - picnic groves and pavilions sited at the ends of urban trolley lines. By the early 1900s there were an estimated 2,000 such amusement parks in the United States. San Francisco had one of the best. Adolph Sutro made his money designing ventilation and drainage tunnels for mines and every dollar in went out to buy land. At one time Sutro owned one of every 10 acres in San Francisco. His pet project was the Cliff House, a Victorian showcase for dining and entertaining, with a public bathhouse below. The Sutro Baths comprised the largest indoor swimming complex in the world. There were seven saltwater pools which Sutro ingenuously designed to be emptied and refilled every day from the tides. The pools were lined with slides and diving boards. There could be as many as 10,000 swimmers at one time in the Baths - 20,000 bathing suits and 40,000 towels were on hand to rent. There was a natural history museum, bandshell and eating pavilions. And Sutro enclosed the entire three-acre pleasure palace under glass. To insure the Sutro Baths were accessible to all Sutro charged only a nickel to ride the train and 25 cents to swim all day, suit and towel included. The bathing park never made Adolph Sutro any money but they propelled him into the mayor's office in 1895. His empire unraveled with his death three years later and the wondrous Sutro Baths were largely forgotten when fire swept the building away in 1966. The concrete foundations remain a popular curiosity in the Golden Gate National Recreation Area.

Folsom Powerhouse
Folsom
1895

By the 1890s it was clear that the future of power in America would be electricity. But how would it be transmitted? Thomas Edison's pioneering power plants ran on direct current (DC). With low voltages direct current was safe but difficult to scale. George Westinghouse was promoting alternating current (AC) which, while more fickle, could send electricity much further than Edison's model. Victory in the "Battle of the Currents" for Westinghouse was sealed when he won the bid to provide electricity for the Columbian Exposition in Chicago in 1893. Ultimately 95% of all electricity customers would use alternating current. One of the first places, improbably, that AC power would be transmitted was on the American River. The four Folsom generators were too enormous (30 tons each) to be carried by rail so they had to travel 19,000 miles by ship around Cape Horn. The turbines in the powerhouse fired up the first electricity on July 13, 1895, sending power 22 miles to Sacramento - one of the longest transmission lines yet built in America. The landmark Folsom Powerhouse provided 57 years of continuous service before it was turned over to the State of California as an historic site.

Del Monte Golf Course
Monterey
1897

In 1890 it was possible to count the number of golf courses in the United States on one hand. By the time the new century arrived there were over 1,000; California boasted nearly 100. The golf craze in Northern California launched with the Burlingame Golf Club in 1893, just one year after Englishman Charles E. Maud laid out the state's first nine holes at Pedley Farms in Riverside, east of Los Angeles. Charles Crocker, shedding Southern Pacific Railroad money, established the Del Monte resort in 1880. To supplement one of the finest Victorian-era hotels on the West Coast the Del Monte grounds included walking paths, polo fields, a race track, and eventually a golf course laid out by Maud. The scenic 17-Mile Drive was laid out along the coastline for carriages with the beginning and ending points at the hotel. In 1903 the course was the first in California to expand to a regulation 18 holes and hosted the first championships of the newly formed Pacific Coast Golf Association. The Del Monte Golf Course, however, would be overshadowed after 1919 when the Pebble Beach Golf Links, on every golfer's Mount Rushmore of American courses, was added to the property. Of Northern California's pioneering golf courses only Del Monte and the Presidio Golf Club (1895) remain in operation. In 2017 the tiny greens and punishing rough of the Del Monte Golf Course hosted the prestigious U.S. Hickory Open Championship, captured by Nico Bollini.

Ferry Building
San Francisco
1898

Much of today's San Francisco Financial District was under water during Spanish and Mexican rule. The Bay shoreline originally ended at Battery Street but with the American annexation and the California Gold Rush about five blocks worth of new city ground was created all the way to the Embarcadero. Sand hills as tall as ten men once stood here and they were leveled and the sand used for fill. Gold Rush money quickly made Market Street the "Wall Street of the West." Anchoring Market Street is the San Francisco ferry terminal that survived the 1906 earthquake while all else in the neighborhood collapsed or burned. Until the completion of the Bay Bridge and Golden Gate Bridge in the 1930s it was the second busiest transit terminal in the world, behind only London's Charing Cross Station. The clock tower that lords over the structure was modeled after the 12th century Giralda bell tower in Seville, Spain.

Latitude Observatory
Ukiah
1899

International scientific co-operation among nations was practically un-heard of in the 19th century. One of the outliers was the International Geodetic Association, a private consortium based in Germany. After a German scientist proved that the earth wobbles on its polar axis in 1899 the group sought to measure variations in latitude caused by the fluctuations. Six Polar Motion Service observatories were established around the world: one in Japan, one in Russian Turkestan, one in Italy and three in the United States, including this one in Ukiah. The tiny structure was large enough to house a powerful German telescope and the gable roof opened to permit recordings from twelve groups of stars. World War I put a crimp in congenial scientific proceedings but when hostilities subsided the program geared up again. The Lat-itude Observatory continued with regular recordings here until 1982 when it was replaced by satellite transmissions. The building has been restored as part of a city park that interprets the site.

Cannery Row
Monterey
1902

"Cannery Row in Monterey in California is a poem, a stink, a grating noise, a quality of light, a tone, a habit, a nostalgia, a dream." That is how Salinas native John Steinbeck inserted the Monterey waterfront of fish packing plants and flophouses into the American imagination in his novel *Cannery Row* in 1945. By that time the sardine fishery in Monterey Bay was already in decline; when Nick Nolte and Debra Winger starred as as Doc and Suzy in the Hollywood version in 1984, it would be collapsed. Canning sardines began in San Francisco in 1889 and Monterey in 1902. By the 1920s sardines were the most important and largest commercial fishery in California. Too much demand - not just by humans but chickens and plants, shifting water temperatures, and ineffective government oversight conspired to destroy the industry. But unlike similar decaying American waterfronts Steinbeck had given Monterey a valuable name recognition and a catchy name. In the 1970s local entrepreneurs used that cachet to open two restaurants under the banner of the Cannery Row Company. The fish trawlers were replaced by tour buses and the waterfront Steinbeck had said was occupied mostly by "whores, pimps, gamblers, and sons of bitches" became the number one visitor destination on California's Central Coast.

SF Lawn Bowling Club
San Francisco
1902

The ancient game of bowls was so popular in England that in 1361 King Edward III had to ban the sport because too many men were on the greens and not practicing their archery, which was critical to national defense. Two hundred years later Henry VIII decreed that common folk were forbidden to play at all, save for on Christmas. History books tell us that the Puritans came to the New World to practice religious freedom but it may well have been to pursue their lawn bowling passion - there was a green on the Boston Common as early as the 1630s. When the Americans overthrew English rule it seems they told King George to pack up and take his bowls with him as well as the game disappeared. Bowling in early America was Ninepins, a game more suited to the American disposition as the bowling balls were used to smash down pins and not the subtle skill of nestling up close to a "jack." In the late 1800s lawn bowling in the United States began making a comeback in private clubs here and there. In Golden Gate Park a public green was constructed to accommodate the San Francisco Scottish Bowling Club. Seem the Scots, barely governable on their best days, had never taken the English ban on bowls seriously and recent Scottish immigrants to the city were eager to resume their games. Today the country's oldest lawn bowling club thrives in its original location; the single-story Edwardian-style clubhouse was added in 1915.

LeConte Lodge
Curry Village
1904

The Sierra Club and Yosemite National Park have been intertwined since 1889 when writer Robert Underwood Johnson and naturalist John Muir camped out at Soda Springs in the Tuolumne Meadows and sketched out plans for America's first conservation protection organization. Yosemite became America's third national park in 1890 but Yosemite Valley and the Mariposa Grove of Giant Sequoias, which had been under federal protection since 1864, were returned to the state. Lest anyone misconstrue the new Sierra Club's mission its logo depicted a giant sequoia and the Half Dome rock formation. As the Club lobbied for the expansion of the park a reading room and information center were set up in a cottage in the Yosemite Valley. In 1902 Club members were taxed $1.00 to fund its first permanent facility that would be named for charter member Joseph LeConte. LeConte had suffered a heart attack the previous year at the age of 78 as he was preparing to join the first of the Club's annual wilderness excursions known as the High Trips. The iconic trips continued into the 1970s when it was decided that groups of up to 200 were negatively impacting the mountain environments. In 1906, thanks in part to a three-day camping trip by Muir and President Theodore Roosevelt, the Yosemite Valley and the Mariposa Grove became permanent parts of Yosemite National Park. The LeConte Memorial Lodge was moved to its current location in 1919 where it houses the Club's Yosemite Conservation Heritage Center.

El Campanil
Oakland
1904

A San Francisco native, Julia Morgan seemed destined to be a pioneering woman in civil engineering when she took her degree from the University of California at Berkeley. Instead she caught the architecture bug and took aim at the most celebrated design school in the world - the Ecole des Beaux-Arts in Paris. She sailed to France and knocked on the door and was refused entrance; the school had never admitted a woman before. Morgan found work as a drafter and after a two-year wait was accepted for study. After leaving Paris in 1902 with a certificate in architecture Morgan, now 30 years old, returned home and became the first woman licensed as an architect in California. One of her first commissions came for a 72-foot bell tower on the campus of Mills College. Morgan used reinforced concrete in the structure, virtually unheard of at the time. Two years later as the Bay Area lay in destruction following a 7.9 magnitude earthquake, El Campanil stood tall, relatively unscathed. Morgan's career skyrocketed. She would go on to design 800 buildings, mostly in the Golden State and Hawaii. Her most famous clients were the Hearst family who she worked with for three generations, including designing the Hearst Castle in San Simeon. Long after her death in 1957 Julia Morgan was inducted into the California Hall of Fame and given the highest award the American Institute of Architects can bestow, the AIA Gold Medal. As usual she was the first woman so honored.

Walters Ranch Hop Kiln
Healdsburg
1905

Really, is there any crop than can not be grown in California? What about hops, you say. There are barely 100 acres of hops in cultivation in the Golden State. That was not always the case. Wilson Flint is said to have planted the first hops in California soil from rootstocks brought out of New England in 1855. It wasn't long before Sonoma County hops were grabbing a big chunk of the national market from growers in Wisconsin and Michigan. In the early 1900s if you were looking for hops you were looking in the Golden State. Giant kilns to process hops flowers were common sights on California farms. Hops were an especially labor-intensive crop to harvest and when Florian Dauenhauer, a Santa Rosa tinkerer, invented an automated picking machine one might expect the contraption to be greeted with hosannas. Instead the hop picking machine helped launch large operations in Oregon and Washington to the detriment of the many small family-run hops farms in California. As late as the 1960s California still commanded 20% of the national hops market but most of the Sonoma fields were being turned over to wine grapes. After all, wine grapes are sexier than hops. But you get the feeling if the Golden State ever wanted to snatch back the hops market from its Northwestern neighbors it could do so.

Lodi Arch

Lodi
1907

In 1907 Lodi was a small community of 2,000 that had just incorporated as a city. The townsfolk were eagerly anticipating the arrival of the new Southern Pacific Railroad passenger station that the *Stockton Daily Evening Record* promised would be "one of the prettiest depots and surroundings that can be found anywhere in the State." Optimism was everywhere and it made sense that it was time to celebrate the region's signature grape. As the *Lodi Sentinel* gushed, "Lodi will show to the world what she produces by displaying the real product before their eyes and decorate the town with vines and grapes, making this city resemble a living vineyard as near as possible... Let us show them... Santa Barbara and Pasadena became famous on account of their flowers; oranges made Los Angeles, and fruit made San Jose famous – let grapes make Lodi famous." That grape was a plump, seeded table grape called Flame Tokay that Hungarians used to make "the world's oldest sweet wine." And so was born the Tokay Carnival. The three-day bash featured a mile-long parade, a Wild West show, and 100 exhibit tents in the city park to teach about grapes. The governor came to crown Queen Zinfandel. By all accounts Tokay Carnival was a smashing success. But an encore never appeared. By the 1930s many in the town probably had no idea why Lodi possessed one of the finest Spanish Mission arches to be found anywhere. In 1934 city boosters tried again with the Lodi Grape Festival. Now the official San Joaquin County Fair, the event is still going strong although America celebrates differently these days - Lodi stopped crowning queens in 1981 and interest waned so much in the Grand Parade through the arch that it was sidelined in 2002.

Sing Chong Building
San Francisco
1907

With a start date of 1848, San Francisco's Chinatown is the oldest in North America and the largest Chinese community outside Asia. While San Francisco today might seem unimaginable without Chinatown, residents were forced to fight for the ground several times since its foundation. In the wake of rampant unemployment in the wake of the Panic of 1873 racial tensions in San Francisco flared into full-blown race riots. In response, the Consolidated Chinese Benevolent Association or the Chinese Six Companies was created as a means of providing the community with a unified voice. One of their first battles was over immigration quotas when the United States government passed the Chinese Exclusion Act of 1882, the first of several odious laws targeting the Chinese. Following the 1906 Earthquake Chinese merchants and landowners were aware of plans to move Chinatown off to the remote southern edge of town so they set out to cement their neighborhood in place as a vibrant tourist attraction to "Westerners." The Sing Chong Building was the first to be raised, helping to define a standard for the colorful "Oriental" style of architecture seen in Chinatown going forward.

Gilroy Free Library
Gilroy
1910

When he decided to retire in 1901, while in his mid-60s after building the world's greatest steel works, industrialist Andrew Carnegie met with financier J.P. Morgan to discuss a sale. It was not a difficult negotiation. Morgan asked Carnegie to write down a price. The steel magnate scribbled "400 million" and slid the paper across the table. "Congratulations, Mr. Carnegie," said the banker. "You are now the richest man in the world." That's over $5 billion in 1924 dollars. When Carnegie got his first raise as a teenager working in the offices of the Pennsylvania Railroad - to $35 a month - he wrote years later, "I couldn't imagine what I could ever do with so much money." Now he had to give away $400 million. He only managed to disperse $350 million, with much of the largesse going to construct more than 2,500 public libraries across the world. California received 121 grants to build 142 libraries. Gilroy pocketed $10,000 and turned to William Henry Weeks, a respected architect of schools, to provide a design. Weeks delivered one of his seven "classic Carnegies" in the style of a Greek temple with a central pediment and Doric columns. The building is virtually unchanged as it does duty as a museum today. Andrew Carnegie would later run into J.P. Morgan again, lamenting, "I should have asked for $100 million more." "You would have gotten it," said Morgan.

Immigration Center
Angel Island
1910

Through the 1800s individual states had loose immigration laws but in practice if a newcomer could make it to the American shores the welcome mat was out. That began to change in the 1880s; the first federal immigration station was established at Ellis Island in New York harbor. With the Panama Canal set to open the second station was set up on Angel Island, the second largest island in San Francisco Bay. The expected crush of Europeans traveling through the canal never materialized and most of the arrivals at Angel Island were from Asia. Chinese immigrants were recruited in the mid-1800s when they were needed to build railroads, work in the fields and dig mines. But after the Panic of 1873 the job market for unskilled jobs tightened and Americans sought a way to stem Chinese competition. The result was the national Chinese Exclusion Act of 1882 and additional restrictive policies that followed. Whereas the rejection rate at Ellis Island hovered around 3% in most years at Angel Island it could be 20%. Inspectors saw their job not as processing new arrivals but as enforcing the exclusion laws. As a result the "Ellis Island of the West" morphed into more of a detention center. Still, 175,000 Chinese entered the country through Angel Island before a fire closed the facility in 1940. Now part of a state park the buildings carry on as the Angel Island Immigration Museum.

Tower Hall
San Jose
1911

George Washington Minns was 42 years old in 1855. The Harvard-educated lawyer had sailed from Massachusetts on the clipper ship *Winged Arrow* just the year before but his nascent San Francisco law practice was in tatters. Minns took a job teaching natural sciences in the Union Grammar School. He became obsessed with the role teachers played in shaping the minds of America's youth and in 1857 established the Minns Evening Normal School to train teachers. His students would be the first graduates of what is today the largest public university system in America, dispensing north of 100,000 bachelor's degrees every year. In 1862 the California legislature anointed the Minns school as the California State Normal School, the first in California to receive state funding. The Normal School moved to San Jose in 1871 and other normal schools came on line in Los Angeles (1882), Chico (1887), and San Diego (1897). The California State University, now consisting of 23 campuses, began in 1960. The Spanish Colonial-flavored Tower Hall is the oldest building on the campus of California's oldest public college. It is the third main building at San Jose State - the original burned and second was felled by the 1906 Earthquake.

Looff Carousel
Santa Cruz
1911

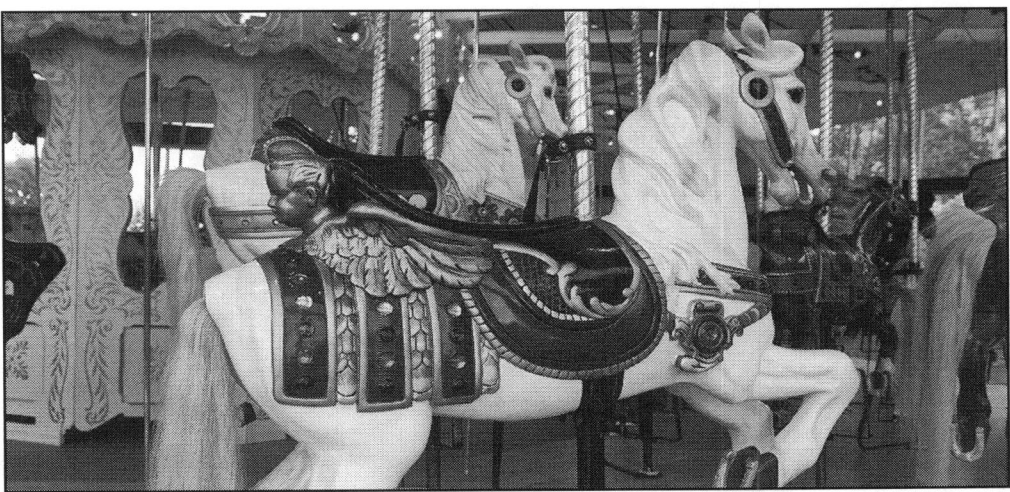

Charles Looff sailed to the United States from Germany in 1872 when he was 18. He found work in New York as a wood carver at a furniture factory and moonlighted as ballroom dance instructor. In his spare time Looff carved wood scraps into animals. In 1876 he arranged the animals on a rotating platform and installed his first merry-go-round in a bathing pavilion at Coney Island; it was the iconic entertainment area's first amusement ride. Looff was in the carousel business. He moved to Rhode Island where he would create more than 40 grand carousels featuring dozens of hand-carved animals. In 1910 Looff packed up for California, leaving behind a carousel in East Providence that would be honored as "The State Jewel of American Folk Art." In Santa Cruz Looff erected a carousel with 73 horse and two chariots for the four-year old amusement park on the boardwalk. Several of those horses flash the master's trademark - an open smile. Music was provided by a rare 342-pipe Ruth and Sohn pipe organ. Today that merry-go-round is the oldest ride in California's oldest surviving amusement park. The rings outside riders can grab still work. The Looff Carousel has taken several star turns in Hollywood movies and operators like to point out the entire tab for the ride was $18,000 - about what a single carved Looff horse would fetch today.

Civic Center
San Francisco
1912

In 1906 a devastating earthquake and subsequent fires decimated San Francisco, destroying more than 28,000 buildings, including the landmark City Hall which had been conceived in 1872 and not fully completed until 1899. To rebuild, city planners embraced the City Beautiful Movement then in vogue that advocated the construction of monumental, classically inspired buildings. To cheerleaders of the philosophy such beautification could promote moral and civic virtue among increasingly diverse populations and create a harmonious social order that would better the quality of life. A lot to ask of architecture. To execute its plan San Francisco went right to the source - Daniel Burnham of Chicago who had conceived that city's World Columbian Exposition in 1893. With a rebuilt City Hall, featuring the world's fifth-largest dome, 19 feet higher than the U.S. Capitol, as its centerpiece the Civic Center assembled government and cultural institutions in orderly, symmetrical buildings grouped around open plazas. It would take three decades for the original plan to be fully realized but when complete, San Francisco boasted one of the most successful renderings of the City Beautiful Movement in the United States.

Fillmore Auditorium
San Francisco
1912

The Fillmore began life as the Majestic Hall whose first tenant was a dancing school. In 1939 the building began a successful run as the Ambassador Roller Skating Rink. In the 1950s Charles Sullivan began booking rhythm-and-blues bands into the space and rechristened the building The Fillmore Auditorium. About that time Bill Graham was returning from the Korea War with a Bronze Star and Purple Heart and going to work in Catskill Mountain resorts as a maître d', an experience that prepared him for managing and promoting his own acts. His first chance came with a benefit concert for the San Francisco Mime Troupe, a group of political satire players. Graham booked space in The Fillmore from Sullivan, who helped him obtain a critical dance permit. Graham began booking paid concerts and when Sullivan, one of the city's most prominent Black businessmen, was shot and killed in 1966, he took over the lease. The Fillmore became ground zero for psychedelic music and the American counter-culture, breaking bands such as the Grateful Dead, Jefferson Airplane and Frank Zappa's the Mothers of Invention. At every concert there was a barrel of Red Delicious apples so concertgoers could feel "like they are coming into my living room." Graham died in a helicopter crash in 1991 at the age of 60 and in the aftermath The Fillmore name has become a national music event franchise.

Cushing Amphitheater
Mill River
1913

The Mountain Play Association put on its first production in a natural amphitheater 2,000 feet up Mount Tamalpais on May 4, 1913. Audience members could either hike eight miles up the mountain or ride "The Crookedest Railroad in the World." During the Great Depression the Civilian Conservation Corps built 4,000 stone seats in the amphitheater from native green serpentine, one of only a handful of places in America the mineral is found. In June 1967 radio station KFRC organized 20 musical acts - most unknown, many to become icons of rock and roll - for a two-day Fantasy Fair and Magic Mountain Music Festival on the Mount Tamalpais summit stage. Tickets were $2.00 and 20,000 were sold for America's first multi-act outdoor rock festival. Unlike its imitators there were no reports of disturbances, despite hours-long waits for school buses to the venue, and festival-goers were said to have left the pristine mountain in the same shape it was the day before. Several of the acts packed their instruments and got ready for the Monterey International Pop Festival the following week at the much larger Monterey County Fairgrounds. Thanks to a documentary film Monterey became much more famous but together the festivals ushered in the "Summer of Love" where tens of thousands of young people in San Francisco's Haight-Asbury neighborhood introduced the world to an anti-Vietnam War, anti-consumerism consciousness.

Pier 43 Ferry Arch
San Francisco
1914

For over 100 years Californians looked across San Francisco Bay and through the Golden Gate and saw nothing but ocean. On the bay was the busiest water transit system in the world. In the late 19th century there were 22 licensed ferry companies delivering passengers to some 30 destinations around the bay. In time they would be joined by another half-dozen that carried only automobiles. By the 1920s the number of companies had shrunk and the boats grew - the flagship of the Northwestern Pacific, *Eureka*, could seat 2,000 passengers with room for another thousand to stand during the crossing. Four dozen ferries were shuttling 250,000 passengers on San Francisco Bay every day. And that didn't include the massive railroad ferries that carried entire trains - the world's largest ferryboat, the *Solano*, was built by the Central Pacific to handle 48 freight cars. Then the bridges came; first a railroad bridge across the Carquinez Strait in 1930 and then the grand highway bridges. Most of the ferry fleet was sold off for use in Washington's Puget Sound. For a spell during the Eisenhower Administration there was no ferry service at all on the bay but high-speed passenger service has since returned. This Beaux Arts arch is all that remains of the ferry terminal on Pier 43 where lumber from giant redwoods, livestock, grain, wine and dairy products would be off-loaded from coastal schooners onto boxcars for distribution by rail around the Bay Area. The Arch building housed weights and pulleys that could raise and lower a 100-foot hinged ramp by as much as eight feet, depending on the tides.

Martis Peak Lookout
Truckee
1914

Every year seems to bring larger and more destructive wildfires to California but fires were once so frequent the state did not bother to start keeping official records until 1932. The relationship between the Golden State and fire changed forever on February 1, 1905 with the creation of the U.S. Forest Service. Almost immediately the federal fire lookout program began a fire suppression campaign to protect the nation's timberlands. The first lookouts were platforms secured in tall trees and accessed by boards nailed to the trunks as ladders. One of the first fire towers constructed was a rickety, 121-foot high contraption spliced together with small poles on Promontory Point in Sitgreaves National Forest in Arizona. It was the tallest fire spotting perch in the country until it was replaced in 1923. Over the years California built 625 fire lookouts; about 2/3 are gone but some four dozen are still staffed even in the age of aerial reconnaissance. Sited at 8,665 feet, Martis Peak received one of the state's earliest lookouts, built by the U.S. Forest Service with a unique pyramid roof before cabs became standardized. The smoke spotters left in the 1970s and the vandals moved in but the lookout just beneath the Martis Peak summit received a do-over in 2001 and is staffed again by volunteers.

Almond Growers Exchange
Sacramento
1915

Almonds were a big deal in Ancient Greece. They were an important trading commodity along China's fabled Silk Road. They showed up in the Book of Numbers in the Bible. But really the world's almond lovers were just waiting for California to be discovered. Every commercial almond in America is grown on the more than one million acres devoted to almond farming in the Golden State. But more importantly 80% of the world's almonds ship from the Central Valley after the tiny treasures are shaken from their trees each October; the subtle-tasting nuts are the state's most valuable export crop. European almond trees were first brought to California by hungry Franciscan padres but the moist Pacific air on the coasts bred nothing but disappointment. Most of the trees ended up as firewood. By the 1850s a handful of cultivars were brought inland to fog-free valleys and tinkering and cross-pollination began. Two varieties stood out - the Nonpareil and the Ne Plus Ultra. By the 1890s statewide production creeped over 200 tons. When the California Almond Growers Exchange organized in 1910 almonds were a minor specialty crop. But those growers were just beginning to experiment with irrigation. In twenty years the yield of the plumper water-fed almonds exceeded 20 million pounds and the exchange with its Blue Diamond brand evolved into the largest nut processing plant on the globe, swallowing 33 city blocks. Almond harvests in the 21st century are counted in the billions of pounds.

Palace of Fine Arts
San Francisco
1915

The United States staged its first World's Fair in 1876 in Philadelphia to honor the centennial of the founding of the nation. Then came another in 1893 in Chicago to commemorate the "Discovery of America" and in 1904 the Louisiana Purchase Exposition in St. Louis marked the 100th anniversary of the acquisition of 828,000 square miles of Middle America. The country's fourth world bash was the Panama-Pacific International Exposition in 1915 to celebrate the opening of the Panama Canal. But to San Franciscans it was also a way to show off how the city had bounced back from the earthquake destruction of a decade before. Somewhat ironically all the buildings were designed to crumble and be carried away after the fair ended. More than 18 million visitors came for the show, strolling through the three miles of waterfront exhibitions and taking in the scientific presentations, sporting events, concerts and art displays. Marveling at structures such as the 435-foot Tower of Jewels encrusted with 100,000 pieces of cut glass it was hard for visitors to believe it was all temporary. As it turned out the promoters did turn a profit on the Exposition but not as much as they hoped so smaller buildings were sold and shipped to other locations by boat. Others were sold to scavengers. In the end only the Palace of Fine Arts, which was always intended to be permanent, is still standing on its original site.

Hoover House
Palo Alto
1920

Three men have left California for the White House, Herbert Hoover in 1928 was the first. The son of a Quaker blacksmith, Hoover was born in Iowa, raised in Oregon, and educated at Stanford University. He may have had the most accomplished resume of anyone to ever become President - revered engineer, leader of the American Relief Administration after World War I coordinating food shipments to millions of starving Europeans, Secretary of Commerce under two administrations in wildly prosperous times. The onset of the Great Depression turned Hoover into a one-term President and he returned to Palo Alto and the only home he and his wife Lou ever knew. She wielded a mean Curriculum Vitae herself. Also a native Iowan, Lou Henry was the first woman at Stanford to graduate with a degree in geology. She spoke six languages and was instrumental in helping establish the Girl Scouts of America. The house was constructed to Lou Henry's designs, with much of it built into a hillside to camouflage its enormity. The eclectic modern appearance foreshadowed the clean lines of the International Style that was on the architectural horizon and is believed to have been inspired by Mrs. Hoover's travels in North Africa. After Lou died in 1944 Hoover donated the house to Stanford where it is now the official residence of the university president. Hoover lived another 20 years, writing books and taking the occasional high level government appointment but not surviving long enough to see 21st century historians rebuild his reputation upon further reflection of the Depression.

O'Shaughnessy Dam
Tuolumne River
1923

Even after more than 100 years conservationists can not say the words "Hetch Hetchy" without a tinge of regret and a shake of the head. Getting safe drinking water to San Franciscans had been a struggle ever since hundreds of thousands of newcomers showed up on the city's doorstep in the 1850s. After the devastation wrought by the 1906 earthquake finding potable water became a crisis. The obvious place to look was the Sierra Mountains and the debate started. The newspapers called these unusual new protesters "nature lovers." Sierra Club president John Muir pled the case for the Hetch Hetchy Valley, "No holier temple has ever been consecrated by the heart of man." All to no avail; the Raker Bill, H.R. 7207, granting San Francisco the right to dam the Hetch Hetchy Valley inside of Yosemite National Park sailed through the House of Representatives. Debate was spirited in the Senate before ultimately passing and Woodrow Wilson signed the law on December 19, 1913. The 430-foot high O'Shaughnessy Dam was finished in 1923, backing up water in the valley for eight miles. Drinking water began arriving in San Francisco in 1934, in the 21st century the city gets 85% of its water from Sierra reservoirs. Conservationists have never stopped agitating for tearing the dam out of the valley. The grassroots campaign to save the Hetch Hetchy was not for naught as Americans were made aware for the first time of what is lost when damming great rivers. Sierra Club-led campaigns have kept dams out of the Grand Canyon, Dinosaur National Park, and elsewhere.

HP Garage
Palo Alto
1924

Economic wags are fond of pointing out that if California were a country it would generate the world's fifth largest economy. There are plenty of sectors that contribute to that - agriculture, finance, aerospace and many more - but in the public imagination there are only two: Hollywood and Silicon Valley. The "Birthplace of Silicon Valley" is tucked off a leafy residential street behind an American Fourquare home built for John Spencer in 1905. Spencer was a physician who waged a successful campaign from the house to become first mayor of Palo Alto in 1909. When Spencer died in 1937 his widow Ione moved to the second floor and rented out the rest of the property. Among the first to sign a lease were David Packard and his bride Lucille and Packard's new business partner, Bill Hewlett. They chose the property specifically for experiments with new electronics products. The first they decided was marketable in 1938 was a radio oscillator they called the 200A. Bud Hawkins, a sound engineer for Walt Disney Studios, bought sight for $71.50 each. Packard lost a coin flip and Hewlett-Packard was in business, moving on from the garage in 1940. HP bought the property and restored the garage where it all began in the early 2000s.

Giant Dipper
Santa Cruz
1924

John Allen, president of the Philadelphia Toboggan Company that had been building roller coasters since 1904, once said, "You don't need a degree in engineering to design roller coasters, you need a degree in psychology." Wooden coasters, do in fact, seem to develop their own personalities, rumbling and vibrating as they seem to battle to stay on the track. Today about 100 wooden roller coasters remain in operation in the United States and the Giant Dipper is the oldest in the Golden State. Frederick Church was replacing a legend when he accepted the job on the Santa Cruz Beach Boardwalk to replace the Thompson's Scenic Railway that had once been the longest coaster in the country. With over a half-mile of track and an initial drop of 65 feet that brings cars to a top speed of 55 mph Church's new ride was described as a "combination earthquake, balloon ascension and aeroplane drop" when it opened. That was 60 million riders ago. Today the Giant Dipper has been recognized as a National Historic Landmark by the National Park Service and a Roller Coaster Landmark by the American Coaster Enthusiasts; it is one of only three remaining working examples of the influential Church's work.

Tribune Tower
Oakland
1924

There was scarcely an Oakland when it was announced that the town would be the western terminus for the Transcontinental Railroad in the 1860s. In 1868, the Central Pacific constructed the a wharf at Oakland Point, the site of today's Port of Oakland. Just six years later the *Oakland Tribune* put out its first editions; the paper set up headquarters here on January 1, 1924. Its landmark building came about in stages once publisher Joseph R. Knowland, one time United States congressman, decided to move operations from the Golden West Hotel five blocks away. The six-story base had been built in 1907 as a Breuner furniture warehouse and showroom and upon this rose the exuberant clock tower designed by Edward T. Foulkes. Before the tower officially opened it received national attention when Harry Houdini was hung upside down in a straightjacket from the ninth floor. Onlookers barely had time to be amazed when Houdini freed himself and escaped in five seconds. The 305-foot tower has appeared on the *Tribune* masthead from the time it opened but the paper was forced to abandon its iconic offices after the 1989 Loma Prieta earthquake.

Kezar Stadium
San Francisco
1925

Spectator sports really began their stranglehold on American culture in the 1920s and if you wanted to be a "major league" city you needed a 50,000-seat stadium. Thanks to Mary Kezar, who wanted to honor her pioneering ancestors, San Francisco got its municipal concrete playground. Kezar Stadium hosted track and field meets, auto racing, cricket, boxing and more. The packed stadium in 1928 for the city championship between San Francisco Polytechnic and Lowell still holds the record for attendance at a Nor-Cal high school football game. Kezar's most storied tenant arrived in 1946 - the San Francisco 49ers of the newly organized All-America Football Conference, which would merge with the National Football League after three seasons in 1949. The Niners never won a championship at Kezar Stadium before leaving for Candlestick Park in 1971, despite the presence of the storied "Million Dollar Backfield" for much of the 1950s. Quarterback Y.A. Tittle, halfbacks Hugh McElhenny and John Henry Johnson, and fullback Joe Perry would all make the Pro Football Hall of Fame - the only complete backfield so honored. The Oakland Raiders also played their first four Americna Football League games at Kezar before moving to Candlestick to finish out the season in 1960. After Kezar was demolished in 1989 more people probably remembered the stadium for its star turn in the Clint Eastwood shoot-em-up *Dirty Harry* than for the exploits of the 49ers. The stadium was rebuilt with cozier confines of 10,000 seats, many of which are now souvenirs salvaged from Candlestick Park when it met its destruction in 2015. The arch overlooking the playing field remembers the original Kezar entrance.

Billy Hebert Field

Stockton

1927

The California Gold Rush lured dreamers from all walks of life. One of them was Alexander Cartwright, a bank clerk and volunteer fireman from New York who is credited with codifying the early rules of baseball - setting the bases 90 feet apart, establishing nine innings as a game, making a team nine players, and more. Cartwright found no success in the gold fields and quickly continued on to Hawaii where he spent the rest of his life. If he had time to organize any baseball games in California there is no record. The Sacramento Base Ball Club played the state's first true games in 1859 and four San Francisco teams formed the state's first league, the Pacific Base Ball League, became in 1878. Shortly thereafter America's Pasttime infiltrated towns and work camps throughout California. One such place was the community named for Commodore Robert Stockton whose naval maneuvers contributed to the capture of California in the Mexican-American War. Stockton won an early California League pennant in 1888 and baseball has been played at these grounds ever since. A proper stadium was constructed in 1927 called Oak Park Field which came to host the Stockton franchise when play began in the modern California League in 1941. After the grandstand burned the current stadium, with a capacity of 6,000, was constructed. By that time the park was named for Billy Hebert, a Stockton native and 22-year old minor league second baseman who died during Japanese shelling during the Battle of Guadalcanal. Hebert is considered to be the first professional ballplayer killed during World War II. The Stockton Ports, who have been affiliated with 11 major league franchises, moved to more modern digs in 2005, leaving the field to the University of the Pacific. The Ports have been the most successful team in the California League, winning 11 titles and finishing runner-up 12 times.

Point Reyes Lifeboat Station
Inverness
1927

Congress established the United States Life-Saving Service (USLSS) in the 1870s. Before that, foundering ships had to rely on being spotted by farmers onshore to come out and offer assistance - if they dared challenge the surf at all. With the new stations regular foot patrols walked the beaches and bluffs scanning the waters, ready to dispatch a boat in an emergency. With thick fogs, battering winds and nasty currents the Pacific Ocean dishes her worst against the granite cliffs of Point Reyes that jabs ten miles into the shipping lanes heading into San Francisco Bay. Before a lighthouse was erected in 1870 it was estimated nearly a million dollars of cargo had sunk to the sea bottom here and no one wanted to guess at the number of lives lost. In 1890 the USLSS came to Point Reyes. Just training the eight-men crews in surf boats cost three lives. In the winter of 1913 the Point Reyes surfmen executed one of the most storied rescues in the annals of the USLSS after the steamer *Samoa* ran aground in high seas. Despite thick fog and potentially lethal timber firing from incoming waves the surfmen rescued all 21 men one at a time using a breeches buoy that was a life preserver ring with an oversize pair of canvas legs attached to a line. Two years later the 270 stations of the Life Saving Service combined with the Revenue Cutter Service to create the U.S. Coast Guard, which abandoned Point Reyes for the safer harbor of Chimney Rock in 1927. The roster of shipwrecks at Point Reyes Peninsula continues to grow but helicopters have replaced rowboats on rescue missions.

Ahwahnee
Yosemite Valley
1927

When conservationist Stephen Mather accepted the appointment as first director of the National Park Service in 1916 he realized his job was a constant tightrope act of protecting America's natural wonders while promoting access for folks to visit. Mather knew that first class amenities in the parks were needed to attract deep-pocketed potential supporters. Yosemite was his favorite park and it merited the best hotel. He tapped Gilbert Stanley Underwood for the job. Underwood had designed lodges in Yellowstone and Bryce Canyon to get ready for the grand jewel of the National Park system. He used the rustic style of architecture based on naturalistic materials such as logs and stone, often dubbed "Parkitecture," for the Ahwahnee Hotel. Since park materials were protected by federal law more than 5,000 tons of granite and 30,000 feet of lumber were hauled on trucks over primitive roads to the site in Yosemite Valley. To reduce the risk of fire the frame was constructed of 1,000 tons of steel and concrete stained to look like wood. The soaring ceilings of the Great Lounge and Dining Room highlighted an interior decorated in Indian themes; after nearly a century the Ahwahnee remains the standard for the Park Service's rustic architecture.

Paramount
Oakland
1931

Timothy Ludwig Pflueger was a leader in the development of Art Deco design in California and created some of the state's most prominent skyscrapers and movie theaters in the 1920s and 1930s. Here Pflueger designed the largest multi-purpose theater on the West Coast with seats for 3,476 patrons. Built during the Great Depression with a price tag of $3 million, the Paramount debuted on December 16, 1931 with a screening of *The False Madonna*, a crime drama of con artists targeting a wealthy blind man. Stars Kay Francis and William "Stage" Boyd were in the audience for the world premiere here. But the Paramount remained open scarcely six months before being sunk by operating costs estimated at $27,000 a week. The building was reconfigured solely as a movie palace after a year being dark and operated until 1970. The Paramount was one of the lucky ones, however, dodging the wrecking ball until the restoration cavalry could arrive to create a live event venue and home for the Oakland East Bay Symphony and the Oakland Ballet.

Bixby Bridge
Big Sur
1932

You don't have to scroll down too far on any list of the most scenic drives in the world to find the Big Sur Highway. Even as California was developing in the 1800s there was no roadbuilding along this stretch of coast. In 1897 John Roberts walked the entire way from San Luis Obispo to Monterey to plot out a route that might benefit his land holdings. Early road building in America was left to private individuals and automobile associations and was not the business of government. One auto tycoon not pleased with the road-building mania was Henry Ford, even though he was selling the most cars of anybody with his $490 Model T. Ford argued that if people got used to private money building roads they would never demand that the government - much more qualified for the job - get involved. As it turned out Ford need not have worried. In 1910 the automobile was a plaything for the rich and there were only 500,000 in the entire country; by 1920 there were eight million cars registered in the United States, one for every 10 adults. The government had no choice but to get involved in constructing new roads. The California legislature approved $1.5 million in 1919 to connect Big Sur to the rest of the world. The trickiest stretch for the new Route 56 was where Bixby Creek cut a canyon to the Pacific. Officials debated an inland route but ultimately opted for the highest single-span arch bridge ever built. The deciding factor was not the magnificent setting but it was cheaper than blasting a tunnel. "One of the best drives on earth" was totally opened in 1937.

Coit Tower
San Francisco
1933

One of the original "Seven Hills" of San Francisco this land was known as High Hill by the Spaniards and Goat Hill by the gold rushers. It became Telegraph Hill when the first telegraph line on the West Coast was erected here in 1853, running eight miles to Point Lobos. About that time Lillie Hitchcock Colt's army surgeon father was bringing the family from North Carolina to "The City by the Bay." She would never leave and left one-third of her estate (about $130,000) "to be expended in an appropriate manner for the purpose of adding to the beauty of the city which I have always loved." That turned out to be a 210-foot Art Deco tower, made of unpainted reinforced concrete, designed by architects Arthur Brown, Jr. and Henry Howard. A team of 25 artists were recruited as part of the Great Depression-era Works Progress Administration (WPA) make-work program to decorate the inside of the new tower. Twenty-seven murals highlighting California themes were installed on the first and second floors. Today the murals represent the greatest collection of WPA art in the United States.

Bell Station
Merced
1933

A high degree of personal interaction between American citizens and their federal government is really only a phenomenon of the past 100 years. Before the income tax and national Prohibition and the Great Depression virtually the only contact regular folks had with their government was with the postal service. So when Franklin Roosevelt began trying things to put Americans back to work in the 1930s one of his main targets was to bring "significant" architecture to small towns via the postal service. Thousands of new post offices were constructed - for many small communities it was the first federal building they ever had in their town. Merced got such a building, a textbook example of the "stripped-down classicism" favored by Depression-era federal architects. One of the many new Washington D.C. departments created during the New Deal was the Section of Fine Arts, tasked with painting locally-themed murals in post offices. Some 1300 post offices received artwork during the 1930s, including more than 50 in California. Whenever possible the Treasury Department used local artists and Merced received work from two, *Vacheros* by Dorothy Puccinelli and Helen Katharine Forbes' interpretation of *Jedediah Smith Crossing the Merced River*. Forbes and Puccinelli collaborated on murals inside the San Francisco Zoo. The post office is said to have been the first named by an Act of Congress named for an employee, Thomas V. Bell who dedicated a half-century to delivering Merced mail. These days the practice has become commonplace with post office naming acts accounting for one in every five or six statutes passed in Congress.

Hangar 1
Sunnyvale
1933

The idea of flying in aircrafts using gas that is less dense than the surrounding air is as old as California. Inventors wished bon voyage to steam-powered airships as early as 1852. Goodyear began building blimps in 1925. Executive Paul Litchfield figured that the airships might do "for persons living inland as do yachts for those living along the seacoast." He envisioned mooring stations at country clubs and private estates. It didn't turn out that way. Instead, blimps became mostly the purview of the military. So it came to be that the U.S. Navy constructed twin airships at Goodyear headquarters in Akron, Ohio, the USS *Akron* and the USS *Mason*. Each was 785 feet long. Needing a Pacific base the Navy selected a recently constructed airfield in Sunnyvale. To house the blimps one of the world's largest freestanding structures, covering eight acres and standing 198 feet high, was constructed. The field would later be named for Rear Admiral William Moffett who perished with 72 of his 75 men off the coast of New Jersey when the *Akron* crashed into the sea. The *Macon* was the next to fly and made it to Sunnyvale. But it too went into the sea, crashing in Monterey Bay in 1935 with the loss of two of the crew. When the German zeppelin *Hindenburg* went up in flames two years later that was the end of dirigible passenger travel. Hangar One with its 200-ton orange peel doors was still used for repairs and there was talk of building rockets but nothing came of it before abandonment came in the 1990s. Google purchased the massive structure in 2014 with a ten-year rehabilitation plan.

Ponderosa Way Bridge
American River
1935

Franklin Roosevelt's greatest contribution to building in California came with the establishment of the Civilian Conservation Corps (CCC) to put young men to work during the Great Depression developing parks and rural roads. Until the program ended with World War II more than two million men (no women were permitted in the program) found employment, housed in government-run camps. Enlistees made $30 a month, $25 of which was sent straight to the families. "Roosevelt's Tree Army" planted an estimated three billion trees. The CCC energized the California State Park system building trails, roads and campsites. The largest CCC effort in the Golden State involved 4,800 workers cutting the Ponderosa Way firebreak and truck trail for 800 miles down the spine of the Sierra Nevada range. The work force was drawn from 28 CCC camps. In addition to completing the greatest fire prevention project ever attempted the Ponderosa Way provided unprecedented recreational access to the California high country. The Parker pony truss bridge over the American River was one of over 1,500 bridges built in the Golden State by the CCC. In 1976 Governor Jerry Brown established the California Civilian Conservation Corps based on the New Deal's most popular Great Depression program. To date more than 120,000 Californians have served in America's oldest and largest conservation corps.

Tule Lake Segregation Center
Newell
1935

In the early morning hours of December 7, 1941 the U.S. Pacific Fleet was attacked by Japanese warcraft in its home port of Pearl Harbor in Honolulu. In little more than three months Public Law 77-503 - better known as the Japanese Internment Bill - became official on March 21, 1942. The law authorized the forced relocation of Japanese American residents - many of them United States citizens - from the western states and the territories of Hawaii and Alaska. Some 120,000 men, women, and children of Japanese descent were separated from their homes and lives and transported to ten hastily constructed internment camps away from the Pacific Coast, two in California. Tule Lake Segregation Center, which had started as a Depression-era CCC camp, was the largest and most controversial as it was set up as a maximum security facility for Japanese Americans who had failed an ambiguously worded "loyalty test." As the population neared 20,000 martial law was imposed. The curfews and mandatory searches ended in January 1944 but so much ill will was generated that citizenships were revoked and mass deportations planned. A class action suit was begun in November 1945 and 23 years later citizenship was restored. President Ronald Reagan would issue a formal apology for wartime "mistakes" that radically changed American lives; Tule Lake is now interpreted as a national monument.

Golden Gate Bridge
San Francisco
1937

John Charles Fremont was one of the most accomplished men of the 19th century - nicknamed "The Pathfinder" for his many explorations in the West, Military Governor of California, U.S. Senator from California, first Republican Party Presidential nominee and more. He also is credited with coining perhaps the most romantic nickname in America - the Golden Gate, supposedly for its resemblance to the harbor at Istanbul, Turkey known as the Golden Horn. Engineers began murmuring about the possibility of bridging the Golden Gate in the early 1900s but the one who could not let the idea go was Joseph Strauss, whose expertise incongruously lay in drawbridges. Not everybody wanted such a bridge. Certainly not the ferry companies that were carrying 60 million customers a year around the bay. The military worried that a bridge would complicate defense ship traffic. But, as is often the case in California, proponents of the auto industry won out. Now all that had to be done was build the longest and tallest suspension bridge the world had ever seen. When the "Wonder of the Modern World" opened it was painted a special shade of International Orange, #C0362C, that is now named for the Golden Gate Bridge. The first motorists to cross paid 50 cents in each direction. Every possible plaudit from "most beautiful" to "most photographed" has been used to describe the bridge, the instantly recognized symbol of California.

Shasta Dam
Shasta
1937

When the first shovel of dirt was turned for the Shasta Dam in the small mining town of Kennett along the Sacramento River under the direction of Chief Engineer Frank Crowe it marked the beginning of one of the most consequential water storage and delivery systems ever constructed. The Central Valley Project would come to include 20 dams and reservoirs in the Sacramento and San Joaquin river basins, 11 power plants and three fish hatcheries. Through 643 miles of canals more than three million acres of the San Joaquin Valley would be irrigated. The soil is so fertile that with fewer than 1% of United States farmland the Central Valley accounts for 8% of American agricultural value and 25% of everything Americans eat. When the spillways opened in 1945 Shasta Dam at 602 feet was second in height only to Crowe's work at Hoover Dam and was regarded as every bit the engineering marvel. Shasta Lake that backs up behind Shasta Dam is California's largest.

Bay Bridge
Oakland
1937

The California Gold Rush in 1849 kickstarted San Francisco into becoming one of the great cities of the world. But not twenty years later that status was in jeopardy. The new Transcontinental Railroad was not crossing the entire country, at least ocean to ocean - it was stopping at Oakland and San Francisco was on the wrong side of the bay. San Franciscans began looking for a transportation link across the bay at that time but it took the emergence of the automobile to make dreams a reality. Automobile registrations exploded in the 1920s and no state became more synonymous with car culture and commuting than California. The impetus for the San Francisco-Oakland Bay Bridge, which came to include three different bridges and a tunnel in its five-mile journey, was that commuter. When the bridge opened the upper of the two decks was reserved solely for automobile traffic. Charles Henry Purcell's vision for the Bay Bridge was so audacious that in 1955 the American Society of Civil Engineers tabbed the complex as one of America's Seven Modern Civil Engineering Wonders.

Fresno Landfill
Fresno
1937

It seemed Benjamin Franklin had an opinion on just about every facet of American life. He suggested that his fellow Philadelphians dig holes and bury their trash. Instead, for most of the next 100 years people just did what they always did - throw trash out the window and let pigs take care of it in the streets. Eventually garbage was collected and dumped on vacant land and spread out for scavengers to pick through. At some point the trash would be burned. In the early 1900s many cities began dumping refuse in tidelands for landfill and incinerators came into widespread use. Fresno was one city that relied on burning trash but when 37-year old Jean Vincenz became commissioner of public works in 1931 he had a different plan - compaction. Vincenz had trenches dug, filled with trash and covered daily with dirt and then compacted. The Fresno model for a "sanitary landfill" became the standard for waste disposal across the country. The Fresno Landfill was not perfect; it was constructed without the liners and containment systems that modern landfills employ and the facility was shut down in 1987 and added to the Environmental Protection Agency's Superfund list of dangerously polluted sites. But never allow perfect to be the enemy of best available option - the Fresno waste disposal system is still the most viable method for dealing with America's trash bin that continues to grow every year. The Fresno Sanitary Landfill has been recognized as a National Historic Landmark.

Aquatic Park Bathhouse
San Francisco
1939

Americans didn't have much use for the beach until Alexander Boardman created the world's first boardwalk in Atlantic City in 1870 to help prevent sand from being dragged into the new resort's destination hotels. As beach vacations began being a thing seawater swimming became the fad of the day, considered a cure-all for whatever was ailing you. The crescent sandy beach that existed at Black Point Cove sprouted hundreds of bathing cabanas that could be rented by the day. For decades recreational clubs lobbied for the area to be designated as an aquatic park against encroaching waterfront development. It took the Great Depression to become a reality. The Works Progress Administration set out to construct a "Palace for the Public" who came to the beach. The Bathhouse was designed in the nautically inspired Streamline Moderne style with porthole windows and curved prows that suggest a beached ocean liner. Inside were showers and dressing rooms for hundreds of swimmers, a restaurant, and an emergency hospital. Thousands flocked to the waterfront for the Grand Opening of the million-dollar showplace. And just like that the public euphoria washed out to sea. Seems the City had decided to lease the Bathhouse to private interests. After kids were turned away sculptor Benjamin Bufano had the statues he was working on moved out to the beach, explaining indignantly, "I would rather have kids playing over my statues than to have drunks stumbling over them." The protest worked. After war duty the Bathhouse became the first private, non-profit Senior Center in the country. Today the Bathhouse is part museum, part concessions stand decorated with spectacular Depression-era murals.

Richmond Shipyards
Richmond
1940

New York-born Henry Kaiser began his working life as a photographer, running his own studio by the time he was 20, in 1902. He took his profits and moved to Washington state to start a paving company, one of the first to use heavy construction machinery. In the 1930s Kaiser's firm was the prime contractor on the Hoover Dam and the Bonneville Dam and the Grand Coulee Dam, the largest concrete structure in the world at the time. Kaiser's was an early voice in supplying relief aid to European victims of German aggression before the United States entered World War II. He built seven shipyards on the West Coast, including four in his backyard at Richmond, to haul cargo for the United States Maritime Commission during the war. Innovative construction techniques enabled Kaiser to build Liberty Ships, as the Ocean-class freighters were known, simply and cheaply. Although designed for only a few years at sea many lasted far longer. By war's end the Kaiser yards could build a ship in two weeks; smaller vessels could be launched in as little as four days. Liberty Ships were an enduring symbol of America's industrial might and so many were built that thousands of female workers were recruited to get the job done. The shipyards closed with the end of the war and Henry Kaiser went off to build automobiles. In 2000 the Richmond Shipyards became site of the Rosie the Riveter World War II Home Front National Historical Park.

V.C. Morris Store
San Francisco
1948

To many, Frank Lloyd Wright is the greatest American architect who ever lived. In a creative career that spanned seven decades Wright was at the forefront of several architecture movements of the 20th century, including the Prairie School of architecture and modern urban planning. Wright was born in 1867, only two years after the Civil War ended and yet his career was so long he designed a house for Marilyn Monroe in the 1950s. Wright's hefty design resume includes over 1,000 structures but scarcely half (532) were actually built. Nearly 400 Wright structures, including more than 280 single-family homes, survive in 37 states, Canada and Japan. Wright was especially busy in the Golden State with over 100 designs. His first commission was for a private residence in Montecito in 1909 but his only San Francisco building did not come for almost four decades, on Maiden lane, one of the city's most elegant shopping promenades. Bricks were seldom seen in San Francisco by this time but Wright eschewed normal storefront display windows and instead lured shoppers inside with a beautifully crafted Romanesque arch in the otherwise solid brick facade. Wright explained he did not want to expose the fine silver, crystal and china of the store. Inside is a spiral rampway that would become iconic in Wright's New York City Guggenheim Museum a decade later.

Rice Bowl
Merced
1948

As auto travel grew increasingly popular so too did the imagination of roadside architecture. Buildings sprouted whose appearance told the tale of their business - coffee pots, donuts, cheese wedges, baskets, chickens, hot dogs. This type of novelty structure is known as mimetic architecture from the Greek word for mimic. The idea was to grab the passing motorist's eye and lure the car off the road. That's what Joe Hong was doing when he constructed his Rice Bowl. No one had to guess what was being served inside. The business closed in the early 2000s but the "rice bowl" remains.

Squaw Valley
Olympic Valley
1949

Alexander Cushing was paging through the newspaper in 1954 when he happened upon an article about the Winter Olympics. At the time the Winter Olympics were mostly a European thing and of little interest in America. The bidding was going to take place to host the 1960 Games and two American cities - Anchorage, Alaska and Reno, Nevada - had expressed interest. Cushing's own resort, Squaw Valley, was only five years old and mostly undeveloped - he had one chair lift, two towropes and a lodge that could handle 50 people - but why couldn't he host the Olympics? After all California's ski heritage went all the way back to the first races in America contested by gold miners in the Sierra Nevadas on 12-foot longboards. Cushing wrangled the bid by selling the International Olympic Committee on the novel idea of creating a facility from scratch specifically for the Winter Games. In addition to the competition venues, roads, hotels, administrative buildings and restaurants all needed to be built. And a sewage system and electric grid. Oh, and the first-ever Olympic Village just for the athletes. Walt Disney, skier and investor in nearby Sugar Bowl Resort, was recruited to run the Pageantry Committee responsible for the opening and closing ceremonies. It all came together for the athletes from 30 countries who competed live on television for the first time in Olympic history. Cushing reaped the biggest rewards as his resort, now known as Palisades Tahoe, is one of the largest skiing complexes in the country.

Greenmeadow
Palo Alto
1949

This is not the story of a single building but 11,000 of them. Joseph Eichler was said to have developed his fondness for Frank Lloyd Wright-styled open floor plans and copious window treatments while he was in the egg-and-butter business and renting one of Wright's Usonian designs. The Usonian was Wright's attempt to bring style to the masses. He never figured it out but Joe Eichler did. When he joined the post-World War II development craze Eichler's architects focused on blending modern architecture with a budget. New urban-ites could move into a $9,600, 1,000-square foot Eichler home for just $800 down. For the next 15 years Eichler Homes defined California Modern with nine major communities in the San Francisco area and three around Los Angles. Eichler's airy living spaces contrasted starkly with the tract housing pioneered in suburban neighbors elsewhere in the 1950s. In 2005 his Greenmeadow and Green Gables housing developments became among the first planned subdivisions in Amer-ica to be listed on the National Register of Historic Places. Inevitably homeowners built onto their California Modern originals so that pris-tine Eichlers these days have become residential collector's items, fetching millions in the market. It is estimated that only about 1 in 10 of the mid-century Eichler Homes exist in their original state.

Jax Truckee Diner
Truckee
1949

Some of the best eating Americans had in the early 1900s was in railroad dining cars, the true "diners." As travel shifted off the rails entrepreneurs sought to replicate the experience with a similar tubular restaurant design. Some early roadside diners were actual railroad cars just taken out of service and hauled to the streets. The Kullman Dining Car Company began in Newark, New Jersey in 1927, manufacturing diners. With innovative materials such as stainless steel and formica, the company became a leader in pre-fab structures and lasted until 2011. This diner, an exemplar of the form, began life in 1949 as the Birmingham Grille on a busy truck route in Chadds Ford, Pennsylvania outside of Philadelphia. It was closed in 1991 and surrounded by towering weeds in an empty lot when San Francisco restaurant entrepreneur Robert Carey uncovered it. Carey paid $45,000 for the diner and another $30,000 to truck it two weeks across the country to this location where it is estimated to be one of less than a thousand original diners remaining in America.

Sunset Headquarters
Menlo Park
1951

Improvements in transportation brought about the rise of national magazines in the late 1800s. Even corporate America jumped into the publishing business. In 1895 John Deere brought out *Furrow* magazine and in 1898 the Southern Pacific Railroad launched *Sunset* to juice ridership on its passenger trains. The first issue cost a nickel but the main value of the magazine to the railroad's bottom line was to disabuse Easterners of the image of the West as a land of stagecoach robbers and rampaging Indians. *Sunset* was synonymous with California from that first issue with the Golden Gate (the bridge was still a pipe dream) on its cover. When the 1906 Earthquake burned the Southern Pacific's San Francisco headquarters staffers made sure to rescue the magazine subscription list from the flames on te way out. Southern Pacific uncoupled *Sunset* in 1914 when people began trading sleeper cars for automobiles and non-promotional work by the likes of Jack London and John Steinbeck began appearing between the covers. The transformation from house organ to mainstream magazine was complete in the 1920s when *Sunset* became the voice for the Western lifestyle. After a lifetime in the big city the magazine walked the walk to a new campus that highlighted themes in the magazine. Headquarters was a rambling single story Mission-style building designed by Cliff May, whose California ranch style homes *Sunset* had been championing since their introduction in 1932. The lush landscape, which often inspired articles and became a tourist attraction in themselves, was created by esteemed Thomas Dolliver Church. Instead of showing how to travel to the West *Sunset* had made the complete journey of how to live in the West.

Laguna Seca Raceway
Salinas
1957

The languid pace of grass-covered hills where horses grazed undisturbed for the better part of 100 years seems an unlikely place to find a motorsports racing mecca. But Laguna Seca is such a place, one of the three foundational road racing circuits in America, alongside Road America in Wisconsin and Lime Rock Park in Connecticut. An easing of gas and rubber rationing in 1944 led to the formation by auto enthusiasts of the Sports Car Club of America (SCCA) and the country zoomed into a road racing boom with the Pebble Beach National Championship Sports Car Road Races leading the way beginning in 1950. In 1955 actor James Dean was piloting his Porsche 550 Spyder from Hollywood to compete when he was killed in a crash at the intersection of California highways 41 and 46 near Cholame. The next year there was a race fatality and officials were demanding a safer race venue. With site advisement from the SCCA, local businessmen raised $1.5 million and the Laguna Seca Raceway, featuring 180 feet of elevation change and nine turns, was completed at Fort Ord in 60 days. The course received instant notoriety for a 450-foot stretch of twisting pavement known as the Corkscrew that plunges drivers down 59 feet at top speeds. To prep the thousands of spectators for the new racing experience cautionary signs were posted around the viewing area to spell out potential danger: "Stay away from the hay bales. They were put there because experts felt that was where a car going wild would hit. Don't try to prove the experts wrong the hard way." The Laguna Seca Raceway legend has only grown from the beginning. In addition to the Hall of Fame racers who have won here non-sports figures from the Grateful Dead to the Pope have performed in the once-placid hills.

Orbit Gas Stations
Sacramento
1963

There is no architectural style better suited for California than Mid-Century Modern Googie. Bred in Los Angeles area restaurants and inspired by the Space Age, the Crayola paint jobs and dynamic shapes of the Googie style spoke of an America with a can-do spirit looking to a future where anything is possible - exactly the same feeling of thousands of Americans who set out to make a new home in the Golden State. Roadside architects were particularly susceptible to the dynamic Atomic Age design. Upswept roofs and rocket-like fins were sure to catch the eye of the passing motorists moving at ever-faster speeds. Ed Ward populated the Sacramento area with spaceship-inspired Orbit gas stations in the 1960s. The Googie fad faded in lockstep with America's interest in the space program after the Apollo moon landing in 1969. Most Googie-designed buildings have since crashed and burned but you can still fill your tank with Orbit gas at some.

Capitol Drive-In
San Jose
1971

Richard Hollingshead began showing outdoor movies in his New Jersey driveway in 1933 with a projector mounted on the hood of his car and a screen pinned to some trees. A radio placed behind the screen provided the sound. He patented his concept for what he called Park-In Theaters. Then came the battles in court to retain exclusive rights to movie drive-ins; when he ultimately lost outdoor screens sprouted everywhere in the 1950s. In car-crazy California the number of screens quadrupled. While the drive-in mania cooled elsewhere by the early 1960s "passion pits" continued to be built in the Golden State. The Capitol opened in 1971, designed by veteran Art Deco commercial architect Vincent Raney. Raney was known for his domed sit-in movie theaters and he constructed a scaled-down outdoor version here. At one time there were more than 5,000 drive-in theaters operating in America; today 95% are gone. The numbers are similar in the Golden State - where once nearly 250 drive-ins operated there are now 15, more or less, depending on that year's economy. The Capitol is now part of the West Wind family of drive-ins that bills itself as "the largest drive-in theater chain in the world" with seven, four in California.

Transamerica Pyramid
San Francisco
1972

San Francisco's race to the sky began in 1890 with the raising of the Golden State's first true skyscraper, the Chronicle Building. Michael Henry de Young, impresario of the *San Francisco Chronicle*, hired the designers of the world's first steel-framed high rise in Chicago, Daniel Burnham and John Wellborn Root, to create his newspaper palace. With a clocktower topping out at 218 feet the still extant Chronicle Building was the tallest on the West Coast. Its reign as San Francisco Sky King didn't last until the new century as the rival *San Francisco Call* went to 310 feet, announcing in the process that their granite and white marble confection "unlike the Chronicle Building will be a beautiful building and a credit to its owner, Claus Spreckels, and worthy of the great paper to be printed within its walls." After new skyscrapers arrived in the 1920s several towers held the title through the decades until William Pereira delivered one of the most recognizable silhouettes on any city skyline with the Transamerica Pyramid. At 850 feet, this was the tallest building west of the Chicago and one of the five tallest in the world when it was completed in 1972. In a nice turn of history, the winged pyramid was constructed on the site of the historic Montgomery Block that was the first four-story building west of the Mississippi River when it was built in 1853. The Transamerica Pyramid enjoyed the longest reign of any San Francisco Sky King until giving way to César Pelli's 970-foot Salesforce Tower in 2017 that capped his long career of designing cloud-scraping buildings.

Sundial Bridge
Redding
2004

Redding fancies itself the "Trails Capital of California" and backs up the boast with 225 miles of trails within 15 miles of downtown. In the 1990s the community set out to construct a centerpiece for the trail system with a pedestrian bridge across the Sacramento River. The City put together a nice $3 million pot of money which seemed like plenty to construct a quaint, old-fashioned covered footbridge. But some thought that would be squandering a moment for Redding to build a true city signature. One thing led to another and the world's most acclaimed modern bridge builder, Spanish architect Santiago Calatrava, was attached to the project. Calatrava delivered "the world's largest sundial" that features a 217-foot angled pylon supporting the cables for the crossing. The deck over the river is composed of translucent glass that emits an aquamarine glow when illuminated at night and causes minimal disturbances to the salmon swimming below. The final price tag was $23.5 million. When unveiled there was grumbling about the cost (although the overrun was picked up by a private foundation) and the bold design in the crunchy Shasta Cascades. But Redding - the sunniest city in the Golden State with over 300 days of sunshine a year - certainly had its signature structure. Just don't try and set your watch to the Sundial Bridge - it is said to be accurate only on the summer solstice and probably not then either.

INDEX OF 100 BUILDINGS

ABOUT THE BROWN SIGN SERIES

So Yo Think You Know the Golden State...A Story of Northern California Told in 100 Buildings is part of our Brown Signs: Celebrating America's Built World series. You can find more titles available on Amazon. Why brown signs? They are, of course, the signs that point us to our heritage and pull us off the road to lead us to America's treasures of the built world.

So, come along and celebrate America's built world with us...

Made in the USA
Middletown, DE
17 March 2024

51080986R00060